Afterwhiles

James Whitcomb Riley

Contents

AFTERWHILES

BY

James Whitcomb Riley

Proem

Where are they-- the Afterwhiles--
Luring us the lengthening miles
Of our lives? Where is the dawn
With the dew across the lawn
Stroked with eager feet the far
Way the hills and valleys are?
Were the sun that smites the frown
Of the eastward-gazer down?
Where the rifted wreaths of mist
O'er us, tinged with amethyst,
Round the mountain's steep defiles?
Where are the afterwhiles?

Afterwhile-- and we will go
Thither, yon, and too and fro--
From the stifling city streets
To the country's cool retreats--
From the riot to the rest
Were hearts beat the placidest:
Afterwhile, and we will fall
Under breezy trees, and loll
In the shade, with thirsty sight
Drinking deep the blue delight
Of the skies that will beguile
Us as children-- afterwhile.

Afterwhile-- and one intends
To be gentler to his friends--,
To walk with them, in the hush
Of still evenings, o'er the plush
Of home-leading fields, and stand
Long at parting, hand in hand:
One, in time, will joy to take
New resolves for some one's sake,
And wear then the look that lies
Clear and pure in other eyes--
We will soothe and reconcile
His own conscience-- afterwhile.

Afterwhile-- we have in view
A far scene to journey to--,
Where the old home is, and where
The old mother waits us there,
Peering, as the time grows late,
Down the old path to the gate--.
How we'll click the latch that locks
In the pinks and hollyhocks,
And leap up the path once more
Where she waits us at the door--!
How we'll greet the dear old smile,
And the warm tears-- afterwhile!

Ah, the endless afterwhiles--!
Leagues on leagues, and miles on miles,
In distance far withdrawn,
Stretching on, and on, and on,
Till the fancy is footsore
And faints in the dust before
The last milestone's granite face,

Hacked with: Here Beginneth Space.
O far glimmering worlds and wings,
Mystic smiles and beckonings,
Lead us through the shadowy aisles
Out into the afterwhiles.

Herr Weiser

Herr Weiser--! Three-score-years-and-ten--,
A hale white rose of his country-men,
Transplanted here in the Hoosier loam,
And blossomy as his German home--
As blossomy and as pure and sweet
As the cool green glen of his calm retreat,
Far withdrawn from the noisy town
Where trade goes clamoring up and down,
Whose fret and fever, and stress and strife,
May not trouble his tranquil life!

Breath of rest, what a balmy gust--!
Quite of the city's heat and dust,
Jostling down by the winding road,
Through the orchard ways of his quaint abode--.
Tether the horse, as we onward fare
Under the pear-trees trailing there,
And thumping the wood bridge at night
With lumps of ripeness and lush delight,
Till the stream, as it maunders on till dawn,
Is powdered and pelted and smiled upon.

Herr Weiser, with his wholesome face,
And the gentle blue of his eyes, and grace

Of unassuming honesty,
Be there to welcome you and me!
And what though the toil of the farm be stopped
And the tireless plans of the place be dropped,
While the prayerful master's knees are set
In beds of pansy and mignonette
And lily and aster and columbine,
Offered in love, as yours and mine--?

What, but a blessing of kindly thought,
Sweet as the breath of forget-me-not--!
What, but a spirit of lustrous love
White as the aster he bends above--!
What, but an odorous memory
Of the dear old man, made known to me
In days demanding a help like his--,
As sweet as the life of the lily is--
As sweet as the soul of a babe, bloom-wise
Born of a lily in paradise.

The Beautiful City

The Beautiful City! Forever
Its rapturous praises resound;
We fain would behold it-- but never
A glimpse of its dory is found:
We slacken our lips at the tender
White breasts of our mothers to hear
Of its marvellous beauty and splendor--;
We see-- but the gleam of a tear!

Yet never the story may tire us--
First graven in symbols of stone--

Rewritten on scrolls of papyrus
And parchment, and scattered and blown
By the winds of the tongues of all nations,
Like a litter of leaves wildly whirled
Down the rack of a hundred translations,
From the earliest lisp of the world.

We compass the earth and the ocean,
From the Orient's uttermost light,
To where the last ripple in motion
Lips hem of the skirt of the night--,
But the Beautiful City evades us--
No spire of it glints in the sun--
No glad-bannered battlement shades us
When all our Journey is done.

Where lies it? We question and listen;
We lean from the mountain, or mast,
And see but dull earth, or the glisten
Of seas inconceivably vast:
The dust of the one blurs our vision,
The glare of the other our brain,
Nor city nor island Elysian
In all of the land or the main!

We kneel in dim fanes where the thunders
Of organs tumultuous roll,
And the longing heart listens and wonders,
And the eyes look aloft from the soul:
But the chanson grows fainter and fainter,
Swoons wholly away and is dead;
AND our eyes only reach where the painter
Has dabbled a saint overhead.

The Beautiful City! O mortal,
Fare hopefully on in thy quest,
Pass down through the green grassy portal
That leads to the Valley of Rest;
There first passed the One who, in pity
Of all thy great yearning, awaits
To point out The Beautiful City,
And loosen the trump at the gates.

Lockerbie Street

Such a dear little street it is, nestled away
From the noise of the city and heat of the day,
In cool shady coverts of whispering trees,
With their leaves lifted up to shake hands with the breeze
Which in all its wide wanderings never may meet
With a resting-place fairer than Lockerbie street!

There is such a relief, from the clangor and din
Of the heart of the town, to go loitering in
Through the dim, narrow walks, with the sheltering shade
Of the trees waving over the long promenade,
And littering lightly the ways of our feet
With the gold of the sunshine of Lockerbie street.

And the nights that come down the dark pathways of dusk,
With the stars in their tresses, and odors of musk
In their moon-woven raiments, bespangled with dews,
And looped up with lilies for lovers to use
In the songs that they sing to the tinkle and beat
Of their sweet serenadings through Lockerbie street.

O my Lockerbie street! You are fair to be seen--
Be it noon of the day, or the rare and serene
Afternoon of the night-- you are one to my heart,
And I love you above all the phrases of art,
For no language could frame and no lips could repeat
My rhyme-haunted raptures of Lockerbie street.

Das Krist Kindel

I had fed the fire and stirred it, till the sparkles in delight
Snapped their saucy little fingers at the chill December night;
And in dressing-gown and slippers, I had tilted back "my throne--"
The old split-bottomed rocker-- and was musing all alone.

I could hear the hungry Winter prowling round the outer door,
And the tread of muffled footsteps on the white piazza floor;
But the sounds came to me only as the murmur of a stream
That mingled with the current of a lazy-flowing dream.

Like a fragrant incense rising, curled the smoke of my cigar,
With the lamplight gleaming through it like a mist-enfolded star--;
And as I gazed, the vapor like a curtain rolled away,
With a sound of bells that tinkled, and the clatter of a sleigh.

And in a vision, painted like a picture in the air,
I saw the elfish figure, of a man with frosty hair--
A quaint old man that chuckled with a laugh as he appeared,
And with ruddy cheeks like embers in the ashes of his beard.

He poised himself grotesquely, in an attitude of mirth,
On a damask-covered hassock that was sitting on the hearth;
And at a magic signal of his stubbly little thumb,

I saw the fireplace changing to a bright proscenium.

And looking there, I marvelled as I saw a mimic stage
Alive with little actors of a very tender age;
And some so very tiny that they tottered as they walked,
And lisped and purled and gurgled like the brooklets, when they talked.

And their faces were like lilies, and their eyes like purest dew,
And their tresses like the shadows that the shine is woven through;
And they each had little burdens, and a little tale to tell
Of fairy lore, and giants, and delights delectable.

And they mixed and intermingled, weaving melody with joy,
Till the magic circle clustered round a blooming baby-boy;
And they threw aside their treasures in an ecstasy of glee,
And bent, with dazzled faces and with parted lips, to see.

'Twas a wondrous little fellow, with a dainty double-chin
And chubby-cheeks, and dimples for the smiles to blossom in;
And he looked as ripe and rosy, on his bed of straw and reeds,
As a mellow little pippin that had tumbled in the weeds.

And I saw the happy mother, and a group surrounding her
That knelt with costly presents of frankincense and myrrh;
And I thrilled with awe and wonder, as a murmur on the air
Came drifting o'er the hearing in a melody of prayer--:

By the splendor in the heavens, and the hush upon the sea,
And the majesty of silence reigning over Galilee,
We feel Thy kingly presence, and we humbly bow the knee
And lift our hearts and voices in gratefulness to Thee.

Thy messenger has spoken, and our doubts have fled and gone

As the dark and spectral shadows of the night before the dawn;
And in kindly shelter of the light around us drawn,
We would nestle down forever in the breast we lean upon.

You have given us a shepherd-- You have given us a guide,
And the light of Heaven grew dimmer when You sent him from Your side--,
But he comes to lead Thy children where the gates will open wide
To welcome his returning when his works are glorified.

By the splendor in the heavens, and the hush upon the sea,
And the majesty of silence reigning over Galilee--,
We feel Thy kingly presence, and we humbly bow the knee
And lift our hearts and voices in gratefulness to Thee.

Then the vision, slowly failing, with the words of the refrain,
Fell swooning in the moonlight through the frosty window-pane;
And I heard the clock proclaiming, like an eager sentinel
Who brings the world good tidings--, "It is Christmas-- all is well!"

Anselmo

Years did I vainly seek the good Lord's grace--,
Prayed, fasted, and did penance dire and dread;
Did kneel, with bleeding knees and rainy face,
And mouth the dust, with ashes on my head;
Yea, still with knotted scourge the flesh I flayed,
Rent fresh the wounds, and moaned and shrieked insanely;
And froth oozed with the pleadings that I made,
And yet I prayed on vainly, vainly, vainly!

A time, from out of swoon I lifted eye,
To find a wretched outcast, gray and grim,

Bathing my brow, with many a pitying sigh,
And I did pray God's grace might rest on him--.
Then, lo! A gentle voice fell on mine ears--
"Thou shalt not sob in suppliance hereafter;
Take up thy prayers and wring them dry of tears,
And lift them, white and pure with love and laughter!"

So is it now for all men else I pray;
So is it I am blest and glad alway.

A Home-Made Fairy Tale

Bud, come here to your uncle a spell,
And I'll tell you something you mustn't tell--
For it's a secret and shore-'nuf true,
And maybe I oughtn't to tell it to you--!
But out in the garden, under the shade
Of the apple-trees, where we romped and played
Till the moon was up, and you thought I'd gone
Fast asleep--, That was all put on!
For I was a-watchin' something queer
Goin' on there in the grass, my dear--!
'Way down deep in it, there I see
A little dude-Fairy who winked at me,
And snapped his fingers, and laughed as low
And fine as the whine of a mus-kee-to!
I kept still-- watchin' him closer-- and
I noticed a little guitar in his hand,
Which he leant 'ginst a little dead bee-- and laid
His cigarette down on a clean grass-blade,
And then climbed up on the shell of a snail--
Carefully dusting his swallowtail--

And pulling up, by a waxed web-thread,
This little guitar, you remember. I said!
And there he trinkled and trilled a tune--,
"My Love, so Fair, Tans in the Moon!"
Till presently, out of the clover-top
He seemed to be singing to, came k'pop!
The purtiest, daintiest Fairy face
In all this world, or any place!
Then the little ser'nader waved his hand,
As much as to say, "We'll excuse you!" and
I heard, as I squinted my eyelids to,
A kiss like the drip of a drop of dew!

The South Wind and the Sun

O The South Wind and the Sun!
How each loved the other one
Full of fancy--- full folly--
Full of jollity and fun!
How they romped and ran about,
Like two boys when school is out,
With glowing face, and lisping lip,
Low laugh, and lifted shout!

And the South Wind-- he was dressed
With a ribbon round his breast
That floated, flapped and fluttered
In a riotous unrest,
And a drapery of mist
From the shoulder and the wrist
Flowing backward with the motion

Of the waving hand he kissed.

And the Sun had on a crown
Wrought of gilded thistle-down,
And a scarf of velvet vapor,
And a ravelled-rainbow gown;
And his tinsel-tangled hair,
Tossed and lost upon the air,
Was glossier and flossier
Than any anywhere.

And the South Wind's eyes were two
Little dancing drops of dew,
As he puffed his cheeks, and pursed his lips,
And blew and blew and blew!
And the Sun's-- like diamond-stone,
Brighter yet than ever known,
As he knit his brows and held his breath,
And shone and shone and shone!

And this pair of merry fays
Wandered through the summer days;
Arm-in-arm they went together
Over heights of morning haze--
Over slanting slopes of lawn
They went on and on and on,
Where the daisies looked like star-tracks
Trailing up and down the dawn.

And where'er they found the top
Of a wheat-stalk droop and lop
They chucked it underneath the chin
And praised the lavish crop,

Till it lifted with the pride
Of the heads it grew beside,
And then the South Wind and the Sun
Went onward satisfied.

Over meadow-lands they tripped,
Where the dandelions dipped
In crimson foam of clover-bloom,
And dripped and dripped and dripped;
And they clinched the bumble-stings,
Gauming honey on their wings,
And bundling them in lily-bells,
With maudlin murmurings.

And the humming-bird that hung
Like a jewel up among
The tilted honeysuckle-horns,
They mesmerized, and swung
In the palpitating air,
Drowsed with odors strange and rare,
And with whispered laughter, slipped away,
And left him hanging there.

And they braided blades of grass
Where the truant had to pass;
And they wriggled through the rushes
And the reeds of the morass,
Where they danced, in rapture sweet,
O'er the leaves that laid a street
Of undulant mosaic for
The touches of their feet.

By the brook with mossy brink

Where the cattle came to drink.
They trilled and piped and whistled
With the thrush and bobolink,
Till the kine in listless pause,
Switched their tails in mute applause,
With lifted heads and dreamy eyes,
And bubble-dripping jaws.

And where the melons grew,
Streaked with yellow, green and blue
These jolly sprites went wandering
Through spangled paths of dew;
And the melons, here and there,
They made love to, everywhere
Turning their pink souls to crimson
With caresses fond and fair.

Over orchard walls they went,
Where the fruited boughs were bent
Till they brushed the sward beneath them
Where the shine and shadow blent;
And the great green pear they shook
Till the sallow hue forsook
Its features, and the gleam of gold
Laughed out in every look.

And they stroked the downy cheek
Of the peach, and smoothed it sleek,
And flushed it into splendor;
And with many an elfish freak,
Gave the russet's rust a wipe--
Prankt the rambo with a stripe,
And the wine-sap blushed its reddest

As they spanked the pippins ripe.

Through the woven ambuscade
That the twining vines had made,
They found the grapes, in clusters,
Drinking up the shine and shade--
Plumpt like tiny skins of wine,
With a vintage so divine
That the tongue of fancy tingled
With the tang of muscadine.

And the golden-banded bees,
Droning o'er the flowery leas,
They bridled, reigned, and rode away
Across the fragrant breeze,
Till in hollow oak and elm
They had groomed and stabled them
In waxen stalls oozed with dews
Of rose and lily-stem.

Where the dusty highway leads,
High above the wayside weeds
They sowed the air with butterflies
Like blooming flower-seeds,
Till the dull grasshopper sprung
Half a man's height up, and hung
Tranced in the heat, with whirring wings,
And sung and sung and sung!

And they loitered, hand in hand,
Where the snipe along the sand
Of the river ran to meet them
As the ripple meets the land,

Till the dragon-fly, in light
Gauzy armor, burnished bright,
Came tilting down the waters
In a wild, bewildered flight.

And they heard the killdee's call,
And afar, the waterfall,
But the rustle of a falling leaf
They heard above it all;
And the trailing willow crept
Deeper in the tide that swept
The leafy shallop to the shore,
And wept and wept and wept!

And the fairy vessel veered
From its moorings-- tacked and steered
For the centre of the current
Sailed away and disappeared:
And the burthen that it bore
From the long-enchanted shore--
"Alas! The South Wind and the Sun!"
I murmur evermore.

For the South Wind and the Sun,
Each so loves the other one,
For all his jolly folly
And frivolity and fun,
That our love for them they weigh
As their fickle fancies may,
And when at last we love them most,
They laugh and sail away.

The Lost Kiss

I put by the half-written poem,
While the pen, idly trailed in my hand,
Writes on--, "Had I words to complete it,
Who'd read it, or who'd understand?"
But the little bare feet on the stairway,
And the faint, smothered laugh in the hall,
And the eerie-low lisp on the silence,
Cry up to me over it all.

So I gather it up-- where was broken
The tear-faded thread of my theme,
Telling how, as one night I sat writing,
A fairy broke in on my dream,
A little inquisitive fairy--
My own little girl, with the gold
Of the sun in her hair, and the dewy
Blue eyes of the fairies of old.

'Twas the dear little girl that I scolded--
"For was it a moment like this,"
I said, "when she knew I was busy,
To come romping in for a kiss--?
Come rowdying up from her mother,
And clamoring there at my knee
For 'One 'ittle kiss for my dolly,
And one 'ittle uzzer for me!"

God pity, the heart that repelled her,
And the cold hand that turned her away,
And take, from the lips that denied her,

This answerless prayer of to-day!
Take Lord, from my mem'ry forever
That pitiful sob of despair,
And the patter and trip of the little bare feet,
And the one piercing cry on the stair!

I put by the half-written poem,
While the pen, idly trailed in my hand
Writes on--, "Had I words to complete it
Who'd read it, or who'd understand?"
But the little bare feet on the stairway,
And the faint, smothered laugh in the hall,
And the eerie-low lisp on the silence,
Cry up to me over it all.

The Sphinx

I know all about the Sphinx--
I know even what she thinks,
Staring with her stony eyes
Up forever at the skies.

For last night I dreamed that she
Told me all the mystery--
Why for aeons mute she sat--:
She was just cut out for that!

If I knew What Poets Know

If I knew what poets know,
Would I write a rhyme
Of the buds that never blow
In the summer-time ?
Would I sing of golden seeds
Springing up in ironweeds?
And of raindrops turned to snow,
If I knew what poets know?

Did I know what poets do,
Would I sing a song
Sadder than the pigeon's coo
When the days are long?
Where I found a heart in pain,
I would make it glad again;
And the false should be the true,
Did I know what poets do.

If I knew what poets know,
I would find a theme
Sweeter than the placid flow
Of the fairest dream:
I would sing of love that lives
On the errors it forgives;
And the world would better grow
If I knew what poets know.

Ike Walton's Prayer

I crave, dear Lord,
No boundless hoard
Of gold and gear,
Nor jewels fine,
Nor lands, nor kine,
Nor treasure-heaps of anything--.
Let but a little hut be mine
Where at the hearthstone I may hear
The cricket sing,
And have the shine
Of one glad woman's eyes to make,
For my poor sake,
Our simple home a place divine--;
Just the wee cot-- the cricket's chirr--
Love and the smiling face of her.

I pray not for
Great riches, nor
For vast estates and castle-halls--,
Give me to hear the bare footfalls
Of children o'er
An oaken floor
New-rinsed with sunshine, or bespread
With but the tiny coverlet
And pillow for the baby's head;
And pray Thou, may
The door stand open and the day
Send ever in a gentle breeze,
With fragrance from the locust-trees,
And drowsy moan of doves, and blur

Of robin-chirps, and drone of bees,
With after-hushes of the stir
Of intermingling sounds, and then
The good-wife and the smile of her
Filling the silences again--
The cricket's call
And the wee cot,
Dear Lord of all,
Deny me not!

I pray not that
Men tremble at
My power of place
And lordly sway--,
I only pray for simple grace
To look my neighbor in the face
Full honestly from day to day--
Yield me his horny palm to hold.
And I'll not pray
For gold--;
The tanned face, garlanded with mirth,
It hath the kingliest smile on earth;
The swart brow, diamonded with sweat,
Hath never need of coronet.
And so I reach,
Dear Lord, to Thee,
And do beseech
Thou givest me
The wee cot, and the cricket's chirr,
Love and the glad sweet face of her!

A Rough Sketch

I caught, for a second, across the crowd--
Just for a second, and barely that--
A face, pox-pitted and evil-browed,
Hid in the shade of a slouch-rim'd hat--
With small gray eyes, of a look as keen
As the long, sharp nose that grew between.

And I said: 'Tis a sketch of Nature's own,
Drawn i' the dark o' the moon, I swear,
On a tatter of Fate that the winds have blown
Hither and thither and everywhere--
With its keen little sinister eyes of gray,
And nose like the beak of a bird of prey!

Our Kind of a Man

1

The kind of a man for you and me!
He faces the world unflinchingly,
And smites, as long as the wrong resists,
With a knuckled faith and force like fists:
He lives the life he is preaching of,
And loves where most is the need of love;
His voice is clear to the deaf man's ears,
And his face sublime through the blind man's tears;
The light shines out where the clouds were dim,
And the widow's prayer goes up for him;
The latch is clicked at the hovel door

And the sick man sees the sun once more,
And out o'er the barren fields he sees
Springing blossoms and waving trees,
Feeling as only the dying may,
That God's own servant has come that way,
Smoothing the path as it still winds on
Through the golden gate where his loved have gone.

2

The kind of a man for me and you!
However little of worth we do
He credits full, and abides in trust
That time will teach us how more is just.
He walks abroad, and he meets all kinds
Of querulous and uneasy minds,
And sympathizing, he shares the pain
Of the doubts that rack us, heart and brain;
And knowing this, as we grasp his hand
We are surely coming to understand!
He looks on sin with pitying eyes--
E'en as the Lord, since Paradise--,
Else, should we read, Though our sins should glow
As scarlet, they shall be white as snow--?
And feeling still, with a grief half glad,
That the bad are as good as the good are bad,
He strikes straight out for the Right-- and he
Is the kind of a man for you and me!

The Harper

Like a drift of faded blossoms
Caught in a slanting rain,
His fingers glimpsed down the strings of his harp
In a tremulous refrain:

Patter and tinkle, and drip and drip!
Ah! But the chords were rainy sweet!
And I closed my eyes and I bit my lip,
As he played there in the street.

Patter, and drip, and tinkle!
And there was the little bed
In the corner of the garret,
And the rafters overhead!

And there was the little window--
Tinkle, and drip, and drip--!
The rain above, and a mother's love,
And God's companionship!

Old Aunt Mary's

Wasn't it pleasant, O brother mine,
In those old days of the lost sunshine
Of youth-- when the Saturday's chores were through,
And the "Sunday's wood" in the kitchen too,
And we went visiting, "me and you,"
Out to Old Aunt Mary's?

It all comes back so clear to-day!
Though I am as bald as you are gray--
Out by the barn-lot, and down the lane,
We patter along in the dust again,
As light as the tips of the drops of the rain,
Out to Old Aunt Mary's!

We cross the pasture, and through the wood
Where the old gray snag of the poplar stood,
Where the hammering "red-heads" hopped awry,
And the buzzard "raised" in the "clearing" sky
And lolled and circled, as we went by
Out to Old Aunt Mary's.

And then in the dust of the road again;
And the teams we met, and the countrymen;
And the long highway, with sunshine spread
As thick as butter on country bread,
Our cares behind, and our hearts ahead
Out to Old Aunt Mary's.

Why, I see her now in the open door,
Where the little gourds grew up the sides and o'er

The clapboard roof--! And her face-- ah, me!
Wasn't it good for a boy to see--
And wasn't it good for a boy to be
Out to Old Aunt Mary's?

The jelly-- the Jam and the marmalade,
And the cherry and quince "preserves" she made!
And the sweet-sour pickles of peach and pear,
With cinnamon in 'em, and all things rare--!
And the more we ate was the more to spare,
Out to Old Aunt Mary's!

And the old spring-house in the cool green gloom
Of the willow-trees--, and the cooler room
Where the swinging-shelves and the crocks were kept--
Where the cream in a golden languor slept
While the waters gurgled and laughed and wept--
Out to Old Aunt Mary's.

And O my brother, so far away,
This is to tell you she waits to-day
To welcome us--: Aunt Mary fell
Asleep this morning, whispering-- "Tell
The boys to come!" And all is well
Out to Old Aunt Mary's.

Illileo

Illileo, the moonlight seemed lost across the vales--
The stars but strewed the azure as an armor's scattered scales;
The airs of night were quiet as the breath of silken sails,
And all your words were sweeter than the notes of nightingales.

Illileo Legardi, in the garden there alone,
With your figure carved of fervor, as the Psyche carved of stone,
There came to me no murmur of the fountain's undertone
So mystically, musically mellow as your own.

You whispered low, Illileo-- so low the leaves were mute,
And the echoes faltered breathless in your voice's vain pursuit;
And there died the distant dalliance of the serenader's lute:
And I held you in my bosom as the husk may hold the fruit.

Illileo, I listened. I believed you. In my bliss,
What were all the worlds above me since I found you thus in this--?
Let them reeling reach to win me-- even Heaven I would miss,
Grasping earthward--! I would cling here, though I clung by just a kiss.

And blossoms should grow odorless-- and lilies all aghast--
And I said the stars should slacken in their paces through the vast,
Ere yet my loyalty should fail enduring to the last--.
So vowed I. It is written. It is changeless as the past.

IIlileo Legardi, in the shade your palace throws
Like a cowl about the singer at your gilded porticos,
A moan goes with the music that may vex the high repose
Of a heart that fades and crumbles as the crimson of a rose.

The King

They rode right out of the morning sun--
A glimmering, glittering cavalcade
Of knights and ladies and every one
In princely sheen arrayed;
And the king of them all, O he rode ahead,
With a helmet of gold, and a plume of red
That spurted about in the breeze and bled
In the bloom of the everglade.

And they rode high over the dewy lawn,
With brave, glad banners of every hue
That rolled in ripples, as they rode on
In splendor, two and two;
And the tinkling links of the golden reins
Of the steeds they rode rang such refrains
As the castanets in a dream of Spain's
Intensest gold and blue.

And they rode and rode; and the steeds they neighed
And pranced, and the sun on their glossy hides
Flickered and lightened and glanced and played
Like the moon on rippling tides;

And their manes were silken, and thick and strong,
And their tails were flossy, and fetlock-long,
And jostled in time to the teeming throng,
And their knightly song besides.

Clank of scabbard and jingle of spur,
And the fluttering sash of the queen went wild

In the wind, and the proud king glanced at her
As one at a wilful child--,
And as knight and lady away they flew,
And the banners flapped, and the falcon too,
And the lances flashed and the bugle blew,
He kissed his hand and smiled.

And then, like a slanting sunlit shower,
The pageant glittered across the plain,
And the turf spun back, and the wildweed flower
Was only a crimson stain.
And a dreamer's eyes they are downward cast,
As he blends these words with the wailing blast:
"It is the King of the Year rides past!"
And Autumn is here again.

A Bride

"O I am weary!" she sighed, as her billowy
Hair she unloosed in a torrent of gold
That rippled and fell o'er a figure as willowy,
Graceful and fair as a goddess of old:
Over her jewels she flung herself drearily,
Crumpled the laces that snowed on her breast,
Crushed with her fingers the lily that wearily
Clung in her hair like a dove in its nest--.
And naught but her shadowy form in the mirror
To kneel in dumb agony down and weep near her!

"Weary--?" Of what? Could we fathom the mystery--?
Lift up the lashes weighed down by her tears
And wash with their dews one white face from her history,

Set like a gem in the red rust of years?
Nothing will rest her-- unless he who died of her
Strayed from his grave, and in place of the groom,
Tipping her face, kneeling there by the side of her,
Drained the old kiss to the dregs of his doom--.
And naught but that shadowy form in the mirror
To heel in dumb agony down and weep near her!

The Dead Lover

Time is so long when a man is dead!
Some one sews; and the room is made
Very clean; and the light is shed
Soft through the window-shade.

Yesterday I thought: "I know
Just how the bells will sound, and how
The friends will talk, and the sermon go,
And the hearse-horse bow and bow!"

This is to-day; and I have no thing
To think of-- nothing whatever to do
But to hear the throb of the pulse of a wing
That wants to fly back to you.

A Song

There is ever a song somewhere, my dear;
There is ever a something sings alway:
There's the song of the lark when the skies are clear,
And the song of the thrush when the skies are gray.
The sunshine showers across the grain,
And the bluebird trills in the orchard tree;
And in and out, when the eaves dip rain,
The swallows are twittering ceaselessly.

There is ever a song somewhere, my dear,
Be the skies above or dark or fair,
There is ever a song that our hearts may hear--
There is ever a song somewhere, my dear
There is ever a song somewhere!

There is ever a song somewhere, my dear,
In the midnight black, or the mid-day blue:
The robin pipes when the sun is here,
And the cricket chirrups the whole night through.
The buds may blow, and the fruit may grow,
And the autumn leaves drop crisp and sear;
But whether the sun, or the rain, or the snow,
There is ever a song somewhere, my dear.

There is ever a song somewhere, my dear,
Be the skies above or dark or fair,
There is ever a song that our hearts may hear--
There is ever a song somewhere, my dear--
There is ever a song somewhere!

When Bessie Died

If from your own the dimpled hands had slipped,
And ne'er would nestle in your palm again;
If the white feet into the grave had tripped--"

When Bessie died--
We braided the brown hair, and tied
It just as her own little hands
Had fastened back the silken strands
A thousand times-- the crimson bit
Of ribbon woven into it
That she had worn with childish pride--
Smoothed down the dainty bow-- and cried
When Bessie died.

When Bessie died--
We drew the nursery blinds aside,
And as the morning in the room
Burst like a primrose into bloom,
Her pet canary's cage we hung
Where she might hear him when he sung--
And yet not any note he tried,
Though she lay listening folded-eyed.

When Bessie died--
We writhed in prayer unsatisfied:
We begged of God, and He did smile
In silence on us all the while;
And we did see Him, through our tears,
Enfolding that fair form of hers,
She laughing back against His love

The kisses had nothing of--
And death to us He still denied,
When Bessie died--
When Bessie died.

The Shower

The landscape, like the awed face of a child,
Grew curiously blurred; a hush of death
Fell on the fields, and in the darkened wild
The zephyr held its breath.

No wavering glamour-work of light and shade
Dappled the shivering surface of the brook;
The frightened ripples in their ambuscade
Of willows thrilled and shook.

The sullen day grew darker, and anon
Dim flashes of pent anger lit the sky;
With rumbling wheels of wrath came rolling on
The storm's artillery.

The cloud above put on its blackest frown,
And then, as with a vengeful cry of pain,
The lightning snatched it, ripped and flung it down
In ravelled shreds of rain:

While I, transfigured by some wondrous art,
Bowed with the thirsty lilies to the sod,
My empty soul brimmed over, and my heart
Drenched with the love of God.

A Life Lesson

There! Little girl; don't cry!
They have broken your doll, I know;
And your tea-set blue,
And your play-house too,
Are things of the long ago;
But childish troubles will soon pass by--.
There! Little girl; don't cry!

There! Little girl; don't cry!
They have broken your slate, I know;
And the glad, wild ways
Of your school-girl days
Are things of the long ago;
But life and love will soon come by--.
There! Little girl; don't cry!

There! Little girl; don't cry!
They have broken your heart, I know;
And the rainbow gleams
Of your youthful dreams
Are things of the long ago;
But heaven holds all for which you sigh--.
There! Little girl; don't cry!

A Scrawl

I want to sing something-- but this is all--
I try and I try, but the rhymes are dull
As though they were damp, and the echoes fall
Limp and unlovable.

Words will not say what I yearn to say--
They will not walk as I want them to,
But they stumble and fall in the path of the way
Of my telling my love for you.

Simply take what the scrawl is worth--
Knowing I love you as sun the sod
On the ripening side of the great round earth
That swings in the smile of God.

Away

I cannot say, and I will not say
That he is dead--. He is just away!

With a cheery smile, and a wave of the hand
He has wandered into an unknown land,

And left us dreaming how very fair
It needs must be, since he lingers there.

And you-- O you, who the wildest yearn
For the old-time step and the glad return--,

Think of him faring on, as dear
In the love of There as the love of Here;

And loyal still, as he gave the blows
Of his warrior-strength to his country's foes--.

Mild and gentle, as he was brave--,
When the sweetest love of his life he gave

To simple things--: Where the violets grew
Blue as the eyes they were likened to,

The touches of his hands have strayed
As reverently as his lips have prayed:

When the little brown thrush that harshly chirred
Was dear to him as the mocking-bird;

And he pitied as much as a man in pain
A writhing honey-bee wet with rain--.

Think of him still as the same, I say:
He is not dead-- he is just away!

Who Bides His Time

Who bides his time, and day by day
Faces defeat full patiently,
And lifts a mirthful roundelay,
However poor his fortunes be--,
He will not fail in any qualm
Of poverty-- the paltry dime

It will grow golden in his palm,
Who bides his time.

Who bides his time-- he tastes the sweet
Of honey in the saltest tear;
And though he fares with slowest feet,
Joy runs to meet him, drawing near;
The birds are heralds of his cause;
And like a never-ending rhyme,
The roadsides bloom in his applause,
Who bides his time.

Who bides his time, and fevers not
In the hot race that none achieves,
Shall wear cool-wreathen laurel, wrought
With crimson berries in the leaves;
And he shall reign a goodly king,
And sway his hand o'er every clime,
With peace writ on his signet-ring,
Who bides his time.

From the Headboard of a Grave in Paraguay

A troth, and a grief, and a blessing,
Disguised them and came this way--,
And one was a promise, and one was a doubt,
And one was a rainy day.

And they met betimes with this maiden,
And the promise it spake and lied,
And the doubt it gibbered and hugged itself,
And the rainy day-- she died.

Laughter Holding Both His Sides

Ay, thou varlet! Laugh away!
All the world's a holiday!
Laugh away, and roar and shout
Till thy hoarse tongue lolleth out!
Bloat thy cheeks, and bulge thine eyes
Unto bursting; pelt thy thighs
With thy swollen palms, and roar
As thou never hast before!
Lustier! Wilt thou! Peal on peal!
Stiflest? Squat and grind thy heel--
Wrestle with thy loins, and then
Wheeze thee whiles, and whoop again!

Fame

1

Once, in a dream, I saw a man,
With haggard face and tangled hair,
And eyes that nursed as wild a care
As gaunt Starvation ever can;
And in his hand he held a wand
Whose magic touch gave life and thought
Unto a form his fancy wrought
And robed with coloring so grand,
It seemed the reflex of some child
Of Heaven, fair and undefiled--
A face of purity and love--
To woo him into worlds above:

And as I gazed with dazzled eyes,
A gleaming smile lit up his lips
As his bright soul from its eclipse
Went flashing into Paradise.
Then tardy Fame came through the door
And found a picture-- nothing more.

2

And once I saw a man alone,
In abject poverty, with hand
Uplifted o'er a block of stone
That took a shape at his command
And smiled upon him, fair and good--
A perfect work of womanhood,
Save that the eyes might never weep,
Nor weary hands be crossed in sleep,
Nor hair that fell from crown to wrist,
Be brushed away, caressed and kissed.
And as in awe I gazed on her,
I saw the sculptor's chisel fall--
I saw him sink, without a moan,
Sink life less at the feet of stone,
And lie there like a worshipper.
Fame crossed the threshold of the hall,
And found a statue-- that was all.

3

And once I saw a man who drew
A gloom about him like cloak,
And wandered aimlessly. The few
Who spoke of him at all, but spoke
Disparagingly of a mind
The Fates had faultily designed:

Too indolent for modern times--
Too fanciful, and full of whims--
For talking to himself in rhymes,
And scrawling never-heard-of hymns,
The idle life to which he clung
Was worthless as the songs he sung!
I saw him, in my vision, filled
With rapture o'er a spray of bloom
The wind threw in his lonely room;
And of the sweet perfume it spilled
He drank to drunkenness, and flung
His long hair back, and laughed and sung
And clapped his hands as children do
At fairy tales they listen to,
While from his flying quill there dripped
Such music on his manuscript
That he who listens to the words
May close his eyes and dream the birds
Are twittering on every hand
A language he can understand.
He journeyed on through life unknown,
Without one friend to call his own;
He tired. No kindly hand to press
The cooling touch of tenderness
Upon his burning brow, nor lift
To his parched lips God's freest gift--
No sympathetic sob or sigh
Of trembling lips-- no sorrowing eye
Looked out through tears to see him die.
And Fame her greenest laurels brought
To crown a head that heeded not.

And this is Fame! A thing indeed,
That only comes when least the need:
The wisest minds of every age
The book of life from page to page
Have searched in vain; each lesson conned
Will promise it the page beyond--
Until the last, when dusk of night
Falls over it, and reason's light
Is smothered by that unknown friend
Who signs his nom de plume, The End.

The Ripest Peach

The ripest peach is highest on the tree--
And so her love, beyond the reach of me,
Is dearest in my sight. Sweet breezes bow
Her heart down to me where I worship now!

She looms aloft where every eye may see
The ripest peach is highest on the tree.
Such fruitage as her love I know, alas!
I may not reach here from the orchard grass.

I drink the sunshine showered past her lips
As roses drain the dewdrop as it drips.
The ripest peach is highest on the tree,
And so mine eyes gaze upward eagerly.

Why-- why do I not turn away in wrath
And pluck some heart here hanging in my path--?
Lover's lower boughs bend with them-- but, ah me!
The ripest peach is highest on the tree!

A Fruit Piece

The afternoon of summer folds
Its warm arms round the marigolds,

And with its gleaming fingers, pets
The watered pinks and violets

That from the casement vases spill,
Over the cottage window-sill,

Their fragrance down the garden walks
Where droop the dry-mouthed hollyhocks.

How vividly the sunshine scrawls
The grape-vine shadows on the walls!

How like a truant swings the breeze
In high boughs of the apple-trees!

The slender "free-stone" lifts aloof,
Full languidly above the roof,

A hoard of fruitage, stamped with gold
And precious mintings manifold.

High up, through curled green leaves, a pear
Hangs hot with ripeness here and there.

Beneath the sagging trellisings,
In lush, lack-lustre clusterings,

Great torpid grapes, all fattened through
With moon and sunshine, shade and dew,

Until their swollen girths express
But forms of limp deliciousness--

Drugged to an indolence divine
With heaven's own sacramental wine.

Their Sweet Sorrow

They meet to say farewell: Their way
Of saying this is hard to say--.
He holds her hand an Instant, wholly
Distressed-- and she unclasps it slowly,

He lends his gaze evasively
Over the printed page that she
Recurs to, with a new-moon shoulder
Glimpsed from the lace-mists that infold her.

The clock, beneath its crystal cup,
Discreetly clicks-- "Quick! Act! Speak up!"
A tension circles both her slender
Wrists-- and her raised eyes flash in splendor,

Even as he feels his dazzled own--.
Then blindingly, round either thrown,
They feel a stress of arms that ever
Strain tremblingly-- and "Never! Never!"

Is whispered brokenly, with half

A sob, like a belated laugh--,
While cloyingly their blurred kiss closes--,
Sweet as the dew's lip to the rose's.

John McKeen

John McKeen, in his rusty dress,
His loosened collar, and swarthy throat,
His face unshaven, and none the less,
His hearty laugh and his wholesomeness,
And the wealth of a workman's vote!

Bring him, O Memory, here once more,
And tilt him back in his Windsor chair
By the kitchen stove, when the day is o'er
And the light of the hearth is across the floor,
And the crickets everywhere!

And let their voices be gladly blent
With a watery jingle of pans and spoons,
And a motherly chirrup of sweet content,
And neighborly gossip and merriment,
And old-time fiddle-tunes!

Tick the clock with a wooden sound,
And fill the hearing with childish glee
Of rhyming riddle, or story found
In the Robinson Crusoe, leather-bound
Old book of the Used-to-be!

John McKeen of the Past! Ah John,
To have grown ambitious in worldly ways--!

To have rolled your shirt-sleeves down, to don
A broadcloth suit, and forgetful, gone
Out on election days!

John ah, John! Did it prove your worth
To yield you the office you still maintain--?
To fill your pockets, but leave the dearth
Of all the happier things on earth
To the hunger of heart and brain?

Under the dusk of your villa trees,
Edging the drives where your blooded span
Paw the pebbles and wait your ease--,
Where are the children about your knees,
And the mirth, and the happy man?

The blinds of your mansion are battened to;
Your faded wife is a close recluse;
And your "finished" daughters will doubtless do
Dutifully all that is willed of you,
And marry as you shall choose--!

But O for the old-home voices, blent
With the watery jingle of pans and spoons,
And the motherly chirrup of glad content,
And neighborly gossip and merriment,
And the old-time fiddle-tunes!

Out of Nazareth

"He shall sleep unscathed of thieves
Who loves Allah and believes."
Thus heard one who shared the tent,
In the far-off Orient,
Of the Bedouin ben Ahrzz--
Nobler never loved the stars
Through the palm-leaves nigh the dim
Dawn his courser neighed to him!

He said: "Let the sands be swarmed
With such thieves as I, and thou
Shalt at morning rise unharmed,
Light as eyelash to the brow
Of thy camel amber-eyed,
Ever munching either side,
Striding still, with nestled knees,
Through the midnight's oases."

"Who can rob thee an thou hast
More than this that thou hast cast
At my feet-- this dust of gold?
Simply this and that, all told!
Hast thou not a treasure of
Such a thing as men call love?"

"Can the dusky band I lead
Rob thee of thy daily need
Of a whiter soul, or steal
What thy lordly prayers reveal?
Who could be enriched of thee

By such hoard of poverty
As thy niggard hand pretends
To dole me-- thy worst of friends?
Therefore shouldst thou pause to bless
One indeed who blesses thee:
Robbing thee, I dispossess
But myself--. Pray thou for me!"

He shall sleep unscathed of thieves
Who loves Allah and believes.

September Dark

    1
The air falls chill;
The whippoorwill
Pipes lonesomely behind the Hill:
The dusk grows dense,
The silence tense;
And lo, the katydids commence.

    2
Through shadowy rifts
Of woodland lifts
The low, slow moon, and upward drifts,
While left and right
The fireflies' light
Swirls eddying in the skirts of Night.

    3
O Cloudland gray
And level lay

Thy mists across the face of Day!
At foot and head,
Above the dead
O Dews, weep on uncomforted!

We To Sigh Instead of Sing

"Rain and rain! And rain and rain!"
Yesterday we muttered
Grimly as the grim refrain
That the thunders uttered:
All the heavens under cloud--
All the sunshine sleeping;
All the grasses limply bowed
With their weight of weeping.

Sigh and sigh! And sigh and sigh!
Never end of sighing;
Rain and rain for our reply--
Hopes half drowned and dying;
Peering through the window-pane,
Naught but endless raining--
Endless sighing, and as vain,
Endlessly complaining,

Shine and shine! And shine and shine!
Ah! To-day the splendor--!
All this glory yours and mine--
God! But God is tender!
We to sigh instead of sing,
Yesterday, in sorrow,
While the Lord was fashioning

This for our To-morrow!

The Blossoms on the Trees

Blossoms crimson, white, or blue,
Purple, pink, and every hue,
From sunny skies, to tintings drowned
In dusky drops of dew,
I praise you all, wherever found,
And love you through and through--;
But, Blossoms On The Trees,
With your breath upon the breeze
There's nothing all the world around
As half as sweet as you!

Could the rhymer only wring
All the sweetness to the lees
Of all the kisses clustering
In juicy Used-to-bes,
To dip his rhymes therein and sing
The blossoms on the trees--,
"O Blossoms on the Trees,"
He would twitter, trill, and coo,
"However sweet, such songs as these
Are not as sweet as you--:
For you are blooming melodies
The eyes may listen to!"

Last Night-- And This

Last night-- how deep the darkness was!
And well I knew its depths, because
I waded it from shore to shore,
Thinking to reach the light no more.

She would not even touch my hand---.
The winds rose and the cedars fanned
The moon out, and the stars fled back
In heaven and hid-- and all was black!

But ah! To-night a summons came,
Signed with a tear-drop for a name,
For as I wondering kissed it, lo
A line beneath it told me so.

And now-- the moon hangs over me
A disk of dazzling brilliancy,
And every star-tip stabs my sights
With splintered glitterings of light!

A Discouraging Model

Just the airiest, fairiest slip of a thing,
With a Gainsborough hat, like a butterfly's wing,
Tilted up at one side with the jauntiest air,
And a knot of red roses sown in under there
Where the shadows are lost in her hair.

Then a cameo face, carven in on a ground
Of that shadowy hair where the roses are wound;
And the gleam of a smile, O as fair and as faint
And as sweet as the master of old used to paint
Round the lips of their favorite saint!

And that lace at her throat-- and fluttering hands
Snowing there, with a grace that no art understands,
The flakes of their touches-- first fluttering at
The bow-- then the roses-- the hair and then that
Little tilt of the Gainsborough hat.

Ah, what artist on earth with a model like this,
Holding not on his palette the tint of a kiss,
Nor a pigment to hint of the hue of her hair
Nor the gold of her smile-- O what artist could dare
To expect a result half so fair?

Back From a Two-years' Sentence

Back from a two-years' sentence!
And though it had been ten,
You think, I were scarred no deeper
In the eyes of my fellow-men.
"My fellow-men--?" Sounds like a satire,
You think-- and I so allow,
Here in my home since childhood,
Yet more than a stranger now!

Pardon--! Not wholly a stranger--,
For I have a wife and child:
That woman has wept for two long years,

And yet last night she smiled--!
Smiled, as I leapt from the platform
Of the midnight train, and then--
All that I knew was that smile of hers,
And our babe in my arms again!

Back from a two-years' sentence--
But I've thought the whole thing through--,
A hint of it came when the bars swung back
And I looked straight up in the blue
Of the blessed skies with my hat off!
O-ho! I've a wife and child:
That woman has wept for two long years,
And yet last night she smiled!

The Wandering Jew

The stars are falling, and the sky
Is like a field of faded flowers;
The winds on weary wings go by;
The moon hides, and the tempest lowers;
And still through every clime and age
I wander on a pilgrimage
That all men know an idle quest,
For that the goal I seek is-- Rest!

I hear the voice of summer streams,
And following, I find the brink
Of cooling springs, with childish dreams
Returning as I bend to drink--
But suddenly, with startled eyes,
My face looks on its grim disguise

Of long gray beard; and so, distressed,
I hasten on, nor taste of rest.

I come upon a merry group
Of children in the dusky wood,
Who answer back the owlet's whoop,
That laughs as it had understood;
And I would pause a little space,
But that each happy blossom-face
Is like to one His hands have blessed
Who sent me forth in search of rest.

Sometimes I fain would stay my feet
In shady lanes, where huddled kine
Couch in the grasses cool and sweet,
And lift their patient eyes to mine;
But I, for thoughts that ever then
Go back to Bethlehem again,
Must needs fare on my weary quest,
And weep for very need of rest.

Is there no end? I plead in vain:
Lost worlds nor living answer me.
Since Pontius Pilate's awful reign
Have I not passed eternity?
Have I not drunk the fetid breath
Of every fevered phase of death,
And come unscathed through every pest
And scourge and plague that promised rest?

Have I not seen the stars go out
That shed their light o'er Galilee,
And mighty kingdoms tossed about

And crumbled clod-like in the sea?
Dead ashes of dead ages blow
And cover me like drifting snow,
And time laughs on as 'twere a jest
That I have any need of rest.

Becalmed

1

Would that the winds might only blow
As they blew in the golden long ago--!
Laden with odors of Orient isles
Where ever and ever the sunshine smiles,
And the bright sands blend with the shady trees,
And the lotus blooms in the midst of these.

2

Warm winds won from the midland vales
To where the tress of the Siren trails
O'er the flossy tip of the mountain phlox
And the bare limbs twined in the crested rocks,
High above as the seagulls flap
Their lopping wings at the thunder-clap.

3

Ah! That the winds might rise and blow
The great surge up from the port below,
Bloating the sad, lank, silken sails
Of the Argo out with the swift, sweet gales
That blew from Colchis when Jason had
His love's full will and his heart was glad--
When Medea's voice was soft and low.
Ah! That the winds might rise and blow!

To Santa Claus

Most tangible of all the gods that be,
O Santa Claus-- our own since Infancy!
As first we scampered to thee-- now, as then,
Take us as children to thy heart again.

Be wholly good to us, just as of old:
As a pleased father, let thine arms infold
Us, homed within the haven of thy love,
And all the cheer and wholesomeness thereof.

Thou lone reality, when O so long
Life's unrealities have wrought us wrong:
Ambition hath allured us--, fame likewise,
And all that promised honor in men's eyes.

Throughout the world's evasions, wiles, and shifts,
Thou only bidest stable as thy gifts--:
A grateful king re-ruleth from thy lap,
Crowned with a little tinselled soldier-cap:

A mighty general-- a nation's pride--
Thou givest again a rocking-horse to ride,
And wildly glad he groweth as the grim
Old jurist with the drum thou givest him:

The sculptor's chisel, at thy mirth's command,
Is as a whistle in his boyish hand;
The painters model fadeth utterly,
And there thou standest--, and he painteth thee--:

Most like a winter pippin, sound and fine
And tingling-red that ripe old face of thine,
Set in thy frosty beard of cheek and chin
As midst the snows the thaws of spring set in.

Ho! Santa Claus-- our own since Infancy--
Most tangible of all the gods that be--!
As first we scampered to thee-- now, as then,
Take us as children to thy heart again.

Where the Children used to Play

The old farm-home is Mother's yet and mine,
And filled it is with plenty and to spare--,
But we are lonely here in life's decline,
Though fortune smiles around us everywhere:
We look across the gold
Of the harvests, as of old--
The corn, the fragrant clover, and the hay;
But most we turn our gaze,
As with eyes of other days,
To the orchard where the children used to play.

O from our life's full measure
And rich hoard of worldly treasure
We often turn our weary eyes away,
And hand in hand we wander
Down the old path winding yonder
To the orchard where the children used to play.

Our sloping pasture-lands are filled with herds;
The barn and granary-bins are bulging o'er;

The grove's a paradise of singing birds--
The woodland brook leaps laughing by the door;
Yet lonely, lonely still,
Let us prosper as we will,
Our old hearts seem so empty everyway--
We can only through a mist
See the faces we have kissed
In the orchard where the children used to play.

O from our life's full measure
And rich hoard of worldly treasure
We often turn our weary eyes away,
And hand in hand we wander
Down the old path winding yonder
To the orchard where the children used to play.

A Glimpse of Pan

I caught but a glimpse of him. Summer was here.
And I strayed from the town and its dust and heat.
And walked in a wood, while the noon was near,
Where the shadows were cool, and the atmosphere
Was misty with fragrances stirred by my feet
From surges of blossoms that billowed sheer
Of the grasses, green and sweet.

And I peered through a vista of leaning tree,
Tressed with long tangles of vines that swept
To the face of a river, that answered these
With vines in the wave like the vines in the breeze,
Till the yearning lips of the ripples crept
And kissed them, with quavering ecstasies,

And wistfully laughed and wept

And there, like a dream in swoon, I swear
I saw Pan lying--, his limbs in the dew
And the shade, and his face in the dazzle and glare
Of the glad sunshine; while everywhere,
Over across, and around him blew
Filmy dragon-flies hither and there,
And little white butterflies, two and two,
In eddies of odorous air.

Sonnets

Pan

This Pan is but an idle god, I guess,
Since all the fair midsummer of my dreams
He loiters listlessly by woody streams,
Soaking the lush glooms up with laziness;
Or drowsing while the maiden-winds caress
Him prankishly, and powder him with gleams
Of sifted sunshine. And he ever seems
Drugged with a joy unutterable-- unless
His low pipes whistle hints of it far out
Across the ripples to the dragon-fly
That like a wind-born blossom blown about,
Drops quiveringly down, as though to die--
Then lifts and wavers on, as if in doubt
Whether to fan his wings or fly without.

Dusk

The frightened herds of clouds across the sky
Trample the sunshine down, and chase the day
Into the dusky forest-lands of gray
And sombre twilight. Far and faint, and high,

The wild goose trails his harrow, with a cry
Sad as the wail of some poor castaway
Who sees a vessel drifting far astray
Of his last hope, and lays him down to die.
The children, riotous from school, grow bold
And quarrel with the wind whose angry gust
Plucks off the summer-hat, and flaps the fold
Of many a crimson cloak, and twirls the dust
In spiral shapes grotesque, and dims the gold
Of gleaming tresses with the blur of rust.

June

O queenly month of indolent repose!
I drink thy breath in sips of rare perfume,
As in thy downy lap of clover-bloom
I nestle like a drowsy child and doze
The lazy hours away. The zephyr throws
The shifting shuttle of the Summer's loom
And weaves a damask-work of gleam and gloom
Before thy listless feet. The lily blows
A bugle-call of fragrance o'er the glade;
And wheeling into ranks, with plume and spear,
Thy harvest-armies gather on parade;
While faint and far away, yet pure and clear,
A voice calls out of alien lands of shade--:
All hail the Peerless Goddess of the Year!

Silence

Thousands of thousands of hushed years ago,
Out on the edge of Chaos, all alone
I stood on peaks of vapor, high upthrown
Above a sea that knew nor ebb nor flow,
Nor any motion won of winds that blow,
Nor any sound of watery wail or moan,
Nor lisp of wave, nor wandering undertone
Of any tide lost in the night below.
So still it was, I mind me, as I laid
My thirsty ear against mine own faint sigh
To drink of that, I sipped it, half afraid
'Twas but the ghost of a dead voice spilled by
The one starved star that tottered through the shade
And came tiptoeing toward me down the sky.

Sleep

Thou drowsy god, whose blurred eyes, half awink
Muse on me--, drifting out upon thy dreams,
I lave my soul as in enchanted streams
Where revelling satyrs pipe along the brink,
And tipsy with the melody they drink,
Uplift their dangling hooves, and down the beams
Of sunshine dance like motes. Thy languor seems
An ocean-depth of love wherein I sink
Like some fond Argonaut, right willingly--,
Because of wooing eyes upturned to mine,
And siren-arms that coil their sorcery

About my neck, with kisses so divine,
The heavens reel above me, and the sea
Swallows and licks its wet lips over me.

Her Hair

The beauty of her hair bewilders me--
Pouring adown the brow, its cloven tide
Swirling about the ears on either side
And storming round the neck tumultuously:
Or like the lights of old antiquity
Through mullioned windows, in cathedrals wide
Spilled moltenly o'er figures deified
In chastest marble, nude of drapery.
And so I love it--. Either unconfined;
Or plaited in close braidings manifold;
Or smoothly drawn; or indolently twined
In careless knots whose coilings come unrolled
At any lightest kiss; or by the wind
Whipped out in flossy ravellings of gold.

Dearth

I hold your trembling hand to-night-- and yet
I may not know what wealth of bliss is mine,
My heart is such a curious design
Of trust and jealousy! Your eyes are wet--
So must I think they jewel some regret--,
And lo, the loving arms that round me twine
Cling only as the tendrils of a vine

Whose fruit has long been gathered: I forget,
While crimson clusters of your kisses press
Their wine out on my lips, my royal fair
Of rapture, since blind fancy needs must guess
They once poured out their sweetness otherwhere,
With fuller flavoring of happiness
Than e'en your broken sobs may now declare.

A Voice From the Farm

It is my dream to have you here with me,
Out of the heated city's dust and din--
Here where the colts have room to gambol in,
And kine to graze, in clover to the knee.
I want to see your wan face happily
Lit with the wholesome smiles that have not been
In use since the old games you used to win
When we pitched horseshoes: And I want to be
At utter loaf with you in this dim land
Of grove and meadow, while the crickets make
Our own talk tedious, and the bat wields
His bulky flight, as we cease converse and
In a dusk like velvet smoothly take
Our way toward home across the dewy fields.

The Serenade

The midnight is not more bewildering
To her drowsed eyes, than to her ears, the sound
Of dim, sweet singing voices, interwound
With purl of flute and subtle twang of string,
Strained through the lattice, where the roses cling
And, with their fragrance, waft the notes around
Her haunted senses. Thirsting beyond bound
Of her slow-yielding dreams, the lilt and swing
Of the mysterious delirious tune,
She drains like some strange opiate, with awed eyes
Upraised against her casement, where aswoon,
The stars fail from her sight, and up the skies
Of alien azure rolls the full round moon
Like some vast bubble blown of summer noon.

Art and Love

He faced his canvas (as a seer whose ken
Pierces the crust of this existence through)
And smiled beyond on that his genius knew
Ere mated with his being. Conscious then
Of his high theme alone, he smiled again
Straight back upon himself in many a hue
And tint, and light and shade, which slowly grew
Enfeatured of a fair girl's face, as when
First time she smiles for love's sake with no fear.
So wrought he, witless that behind him leant
A woman, with old features, dim and sear,

And glamoured eyes that felt the brimming tear,
And with a voice, like some sad instrument,
That sighing said, "I'm dead there; love me here!"

Longfellow

The winds have talked with him confidingly;
The trees have whispered to him; and the night
Hath held him gently as a mother might,
And taught him all sad tones of melody:
The mountains have bowed to him; and the sea,
In clamorous waves, and murmurs exquisite,
Hath told him all her sorrow and delight--
Her legends fair-- her darkest mystery.
His verse blooms like a flower, night and day;
Bees cluster round his rhymes; and twitterings
Of lark and swallow, in an endless May,
Are mingling with the tender songs he sings--.
Nor shall he cease to sing-- in every lay
Of Nature's voice he sings-- and will alway.

Indiana

Our Land-- our Home-- the common home indeed
Of soil-born children and adopted ones--
The stately daughters and the stalwart sons
Of Industry--: All greeting and godspeed!
O home to proudly live for, and if need
Be proudly die for, with the roar of guns
Blent with our latest prayer--. So died men once...

Lo Peace...! As we look on the land They freed--
Its harvests all in ocean-over flow
Poured round autumnal coasts in billowy gold--
Its corn and wine and balmed fruits and flow'rs--,
We know the exaltation that they know
Who now, steadfast inheritors, behold
The Land Elysian, marvelling "This is ours?"

Time

1

The ticking-- ticking-- ticking of the clock--!
That vexed me so last night--! "For though Time keeps
Such drowsy watch," I moaned, "he never sleeps,
But only nods above the world to mock
Its restless occupant, then rudely rock
It as the cradle of a babe that weeps!"
I seemed to see the seconds piled in heaps
Like sand about me; and at every shock
O' the bell, the piled sands were swirled away
As by a desert-storm that swept the earth
Stark as a granary floor, whereon the gray
And mist-bedrizzled moon amidst the dearth
Came crawling, like a sickly child, to lay
Its pale face next mine own and weep for day.

2

Wait for the morning! Ah! We wait indeed
For daylight, we who toss about through stress
Of vacant-armed desires and emptiness
Of all the warm, warm touches that we need,
And the warm kisses upon which we feed

Our famished lips in fancy! May God bless
The starved lips of us with but one caress
Warm as the yearning blood our poor hearts bleed...!
A wild prayer--! Bite thy pillow, praying so--
Toss this side, and whirl that, and moan for dawn;
Let the clock's seconds dribble out their woe,
And Time be drained of sorrow! Long ago
We heard the crowing cock, with answer drawn
As hoarsely sad at throat as sobs... Pray on!

Grant
At Rest-- August 8, 1885

   Sir Launcelot rode overthwart and endlong in a wide forest, and held no
path but as wild adventure led him... And he returned and came again to his
horse, and took off his saddle and his bridle, and let him pasture; and
unlaced his helm, and ungirdled his sword, and laid him down to sleep upon
his shield before the cross. --Age of Chivalary

Grant

What shall we say of the soldier. Grant,
His sword put by and his great soul free?
How shall we cheer him now or chant
His requiem befittingly?
The fields of his conquest now are seen
Ranged no more with his armed men--
But the rank and file of the gold and green
Of the waving grain is there again.

Though his valiant life is a nation's pride,
And his death heroic and half divine,

And our grief as great as the world is wide,
There breaks in speech but a single line--:
We loved him living, revere him dead--!
A silence then on our lips is laid:
We can say no thing that has not been said,
Nor pray one prayer that has not been prayed.

But a spirit within us speaks: and lo,
We lean and listen to wondrous words
That have a sound as of winds that blow,
And the voice of waters and low of herds;
And we hear, as the song flows on serene,
The neigh of horses, and then the beat
Of hooves that skurry o'er pastures green,
And the patter and pad of a boy's bare feet.

A brave lad, wearing a manly brow,
Knit as with problems of grave dispute,
And a face, like the bloom of the orchard bough,
Pink and pallid, but resolute;
And flushed it grows as the clover-bloom,
And fresh it gleams as the morning dew,
As he reins his steed where the quick quails boom
Up from the grasses he races through.

And ho! As he rides what dreams are his?
And what have the breezes to suggest--?
Do they whisper to him of shells that whiz
O'er fields made ruddy with wrongs redressed?
Does the hawk above him an Eagle float?
Does he thrill and his boyish heart beat high,
Hearing the ribbon about his throat
Flap as a Flag as the winds go by?

And does he dream of the Warrior's fame--
This Western boy in his rustic dress?
For in miniature, this is the man that came
Riding out of the Wilderness--!
The selfsame figure-- the knitted brow--
The eyes full steady-- the lips full mute--
And the face, like the bloom of the orchard bough,
Pink and pallid, but resolute.

Ay, this is the man, with features grim
And stoical as the Sphinx's own,
That heard the harsh guns calling him,
As musical as the bugle blown,
When the sweet spring heavens were clouded o'er
With a tempest, glowering and wild,
And our country's flag bowed down before
Its bursting wrath as a stricken child.

Thus, ready mounted and booted and spurred,
He loosed his bridle and dashed away--!
Like a roll of drums were his hoof-beats heard,
Like the shriek of the fife his charger's neigh!
And over his shoulder and backward blown,
We heard his voice, and we saw the sod
Reel, as our wild steeds chased his own
As though hurled on by the hand of God!

And still, in fancy, we see him ride
In the blood-red front of a hundred frays,
His face set stolid, but glorified
As a knight's of the old Arthurian days:
And victor ever as courtly too,
Gently lifting the vanquished foe,

And staying him with a hand as true
As dealt the deadly avenging blow.

So brighter than all of the cluster of stars
Of the flag enshrouding his form to-day,
His face shines forth from the grime of wars
With a glory that shall not pass away:
He rests at last: he has borne his part
Of salutes and salvos and cheers on cheers--
But O the sobs of his country's heart,
And the driving rain of a nations tears!

Old Fashioned Roses

They ain't no style about 'em,
And they're sorto' pale and faded,
Yit the doorway here, without 'em,
Would be lonesomer, and shaded
With a good 'eal blacker shudder
Than the morning-glories makes,
And the sunshine would look sadder
Fer their good old-fashion' sakes.

I like 'em 'cause they kindo'--
Sorto' make a feller like 'em!
And I tell you, when I find a
Bunch out whur the sun kin strike 'em,
It allus sets me thinkin'
O' the ones 'at used to grow
And peek in thro' the chinkin'
O' the cabin, don't you know!

And then I think o' mother,
And how she ust to love 'em--
When they wuzn't any other,
'Less she found 'em up above 'em!
And her eyes, afore she shut 'em,

Whispered with a smile and said
We must pick a bunch and putt 'em
In her hand when she wuz dead.

But as I wuz a-sayin',
They ain't no style about 'em
Very gaudy er displayin',
But I wouldn't be without 'em--,
'Cause I'm happier in these posies,
And the hollyhawks and sich,
Than the hummin'-bird 'at noses
In the roses of the rich.

Griggsby's Station

Pap's got his patent-right, and rich is all creation;
But where's the peace and comfort that we all had before?
Le's go a-visitin' back to Griggsby's Station--
Back where we ust to be so happy and so pore!

The likes of us a-livin' here! It's jest a mortal pity
To see us in this great big house, with cyarpets on the stairs,
And the pump right in the kitchen! And the city! City! City
And nothin' but the city all around us ever'wheres!

Climb clean above the roof and look from the steeple,
And never see a robin, nor a beech or ellum tree!
And right here in ear-shot of at least a thousan' people,
And none that neighbors with us or we want to go and see!

Le's go a-visitin' back to Griggsby's Station--
Back where the latch-strings a-hangin' from the door,

And ever' neighbor round the place is dear as a relation--
Back where we ust to be so happy and so pore!

I want to see the Wiggenses, the whole kit-and-bilin',
A-drivin' up from Shallor Ford to stay the Sunday through;
And I want to see 'em hitchin' at their son-in-law's and pilin'
Out there at 'Lizy Ellen's like they ust to do!

I want to see the piece-quilts the Jones girls is makin';
And I want to pester Laury 'bout their freckled hired hand,
And joke her 'bout the widower she come purt' nigh a-takin',
Till her Pap got his pension 'lowed in time to save his land.

Le's go a-visitin' back to Griggsby's Station--
Back where they's nothin' aggervatin' any more,
Shet away safe in the woods around the old location--
Back where we ust to be so happy and so pore!

I want to see Marindy and he'p her with her sewin',
And hear her talk so lovin' of her man that's dead and gone,
And stand up with Emanuel to show me how he's growin',
And smile as I have saw her 'fore she putt her mournin' on.

And I want to see the Samples, on the old lower eighty,
Where John, our oldest boy, he was tuk and burried-- for
His own sake and Katy's--, and I want to cry with Katy
As she reads all his letters over, writ from The War.

What's in all this grand life and high situation,
And nary pink nor hollyhawk a-bloomin' at the door--?
Le's go a-visitin' back to Griggsby's Station--
Back where we ust to be so happy and so pore!

Knee Deep in June

1

Tell you what I like the best--
'Long about knee-deep in June,
'Bout the time strawberries melts
On the vine--, some afternoon
Like to jes' git out and rest,
And not work at nothin' else!

2

Orchard's where I'd ruther be--
Needn't fence it in fer me--!
Jes' the whole sky overhead,
And the whole airth underneath--
Sorto' so's a man kin breathe
Like he ort, and kindo' has
Elbow-room to keerlessly
Sprawl out len'thways on the grass
Where the shadders thick and soft
As the kivvers on the bed
Mother fixes in the loft
Allus, when they's company!

3

Jes' a-sorto' lazin' there--
S'lazy, 'at you peeks and peer
Through the wavin' leaves above,
Like a feller 'ats in love
And don't know it, ner don't keer!
Ever'thing you hear and see
Got some sort o' interest--

Maybe find a bluebird's nest
Tucked up there conveenently
Fer the boy 'at's ap' to be
Up some other apple-tree!
Watch the swallers skootin' past
'Bout as peert as you could ast;
Er the Bob-white raise and whiz
Where some other's whistle is.

4

Ketch a shadder down below,
And look up to find the crow--
Er a hawk--, away up there
'Pearantly froze in the air--!
Hear the old hen squawk, and squat
Over ever' chick she's got,
Suddent-like--! And she knows where
That-air hawk is, well as you--!
You jes' bet yer life she do--!
Eyes a-glittern' like glass,
Waitin' till he makes a pass!

5

Pee-wees' singin', to express
My opinion, 's second class,
Yit you'll hear 'em more er less;
Sapsucks gittin' down to biz,
Weedin' out the lonesomeness;
Mr. Bluejay, full o' sass,
In them base-ball clothes o' his,
Sportin' round the orchard jes'
Life he owned the premises!
Sun out in the fields kin sizz,

But flat on yer back, I guess,
In the shade's where glory is!
That's jes' what I'd like to do
Stiddy fer a year er two!

6

Plague! Ef they ain't somepin' in
Work 'at kindo' goes ag'in'
My convictions--! 'Long about
Here in June especially--!
Under some old apple-tree,
Jes' a-restin' through and through,
I could git along without
Nothin' else at all to do
Only jes' a-wishin' you
Wuz a-gittin' there like me,
And June was eternity!

7

Lay out there and try to see
Jes' how lazy you kin be--!
Tumble round and souse yer head
In the clover-bloom, er pull
Yer straw hat acrost yer eyes
And peek through it at the skies,
Thinkin' of old chums 'at's dead,
Maybe, smilin' back at you
In betwixt the 'beautiful
Clouds o' gold and white and blue--!
Month a man kin railly love
June, you know, I'm talkin' of!

8

March ain't never nothin' new--!
Aprile's altogether too
Brash fer me! And May-- I jes'
'Bominate its promises--,
Little hints o' sunshine and
Green around the timber-land--
A few blossoms, and a few
Chip-birds, and a sprout er two--,
Drap asleep, and it turns in
'Fore daylight and snows ag'in--!
But when June comes-- Clear my th'oat
With wild honey--! Rench my hair
In the dew! And hold my coat!
Whoop out loud! And th'ow my hat--!
June wants me, and I'm to spare!
Spread them shadders anywhere,
I'll git down and waller there,
And obleeged to you at that!

When The Hearse Comes Back

A thing 'at's 'bout as tryin' as a healthy man kin meet
Is some poor feller's funeral a-joggin' 'long the street:
The slow hearse and the hosses-- slow enough, to say at least,
Fer to even tax the patience of gentleman deceased!
The low scrunch of the gravel-- and the slow grind of the wheels--,
The slow, slow go of ev'ry woe 'at ev'rybody feels!
So I ruther like the contrast when I hear the whip-lash crack
A quickstep fer the hosses,
> When the
> > Hearse
> > > Comes
> > > > Back!

Meet it goin' to'rds the cimet'ry, you'll want to drap yer eyes--
But ef the plumes don't fetch you, it'll ketch you otherwise--
You'll haf to see the caskit, though you'd ort to look away
And 'conomize and save yer sighs fer any other day!
Yer sympathizin' won't wake up the sleeper from his rest--
Yer tears won't thaw them hands o' his 'at's froze acrost his breast!
And this is why-- when airth and sky's a gittin blurred and black--
I like the flash and hurry
> When the
> > Hearse
> > > Comes
> > > > Back!

It's not 'cause I don't 'preciate it ain't no time fer jokes,
Ner 'cause I' got no common human feelin' fer the folks--;
I've went to funerals myse'f, and tuk on some, perhaps--
Fer my hearth's 'bout as mal'able as any other chap's--,

I've buried father, mother-- But I'll haf to jes' git you
To "excuse me," as the feller says--. The p'int I'm drivin' to
Is simply when we're plum broke down and all knocked out o' whack,
It he'ps to shape us up like,
>   When the
>   Hearse
>   Comes
>   Back!

The idy! Wadin round here over shoe-mouth deep in woe,
When they's a graded 'pike o' joy and sunshine don't you know!
When evening strikes the pastur', cows'll pull out fer the bars,
And skittish-like from out the night'll prance the happy stars.
And so when my time comes to die, and I've got ary friend
'At wants expressed my last request-- I'll mebby, rickommend
To drive slow, ef they haf to, goin' 'long the out'ard track,
But I'll smile and say, "You speed 'em
>   When the
>   Hearse
>   Comes
>   Back!"

A Canary At the Farm

Folks has be'n to town, and Sahry
Fetched 'er home a pet canary--,
And of all the blame', contrary,
Aggervatin' things alive!
I love music-- that I love it
When it's free-- and plenty of it--;
But I kindo' git above it,
At a dollar-eighty-five!

Reason's plain as I'm a-sayin'--,
Jes' the idy, now, o' layin'
Out yer money, and a-payin'
Fer a willer-cage and bird,
When the medder-larks is wingin'
Round you, and the woods is ringin'
With the beautifullest singin'
That a mortal ever heard!

Sahry's sot, tho'--. So I tell her
He's a purty little feller,
With his wings o' creamy-yeller,
And his eyes keen as a cat;
And the twitter o' the critter
'Pears to absolutely glitter!
Guess I'll haf to go and git her
A high-priceter cage 'n that!

A Liz Town Humorist

Settin' round the stove, last night,
Down at Wess's store, was me
And Mart Strimples, Tunk, and White,
And Doc Bills, and two er three
Fellers o' the Mudsock tribe
No use tryin' to describe!
And says Doc, he says, says he--,
"Talkin' 'bout good things to eat,
Ripe mushmillon's hard to beat!"

I chawed on. And Mart he 'lowed
Wortermillon beat the mush--.
"Red," he says, "and juicy-- Hush--!
I'll jes' leave it to the crowd!"
Then a Mudsock chap, says he--,
"Punkin's good enough fer me--
Punkin pies, I mean," he says--,
Them beats millons--! What say, Wess?

I chawed on. And Wess says--, "Well,
You jes' fetch that wife of mine
All yer wortermillon-rine--,
And she'll bile it down a spell--
In with sorghum, I suppose,
And what else, Lord only knows--!
But I'm here to tell all hands
Them p'serves meets my demands!"

I chawed on. And White he says--,
"Well, I'll jes' stand, in with Wess--

I'm no hog!" And Tunk says--, "I
Guess I'll pastur' out on pie
With the Mudsock boys!" says he;
"Now what's yourn?" he says to me:
I chawed on-- fer-- quite a spell
Then I speaks up, slow and dry--,
Jes' tobacker!" I-says-I--.
And you'd ort o' heerd 'em yell!

Kingry's Mill

On old Brandywine-- about
Where White's Lots is now laid out,
And the old crick narries down
To the ditch that splits the town--,
Kingry's Mill stood. Hardly see
Where the old dam ust to be;
Shallor, long, dry trought o' grass
Where the old race ust to pass!

That's be'n forty years ago--
Forty years o' frost and snow--
Forty years o' shade and shine
Sence them boyhood-days o' mine--!
All the old landmarks o' town.
Changed about, er rotted down!
Where's the Tanyard? Where's the Still?
Tell me where's old Kingry's Mill?

Don't seem furder back, to me,
I'll be dogg'd! Than yisterd'y,
Since us fellers, in bare feet

And straw hats, went through the wheat,
Cuttin' 'crost the shortest shoot
Fer that-air old ellum root
Jest above the mill-dam-- where
The blame' cars now crosses there!

Through the willers down the crick
We could see the old mill stick
Its red gable up, as if
It jest knowed we'd stol'd the skiff!
See the winders in the sun
Blink like they wuz wonderun'
What the miller ort to do
With sich boys as me and you!

But old Kingry--! Who could fear
That old chap, with all his cheer--?
Leanin' at the window-sill,
Er the half-door o' the mill,
Swoppin' lies, and pokin' fun,
'N jigglin' like his hoppers done--
Laughin' grists o' gold and red
Right out o' the wagon-bed!

What did he keer where we went--?
"Jest keep out o' devilment,
And don't fool around the belts,
Bolts, ner burrs, ner nothin' else
'Bout the blame machinery,
And that's all I ast!" says-ee.
Then we'd climb the stairs, and play
In the bran-bins half the day!

Rickollect the dusty wall,
And the spider-webs, and all!
Rickollect the trimblin' spout
Where the meal come josslln' out--
Stand and comb yer fingers through
The fool-truck an hour er two--
Felt so sorto' warm-like and
Soothin' to a feller's hand!

Climb, high up above the stream,
And "coon" out the wobbly beam
And peek down from out the lof'
Where the weather-boards was off--
Gee-mun-nee! w'y, it takes grit
Even jest to think of it--!
Lookin' 'way down there below
On the worter roarin' so!

Rickollect the flume, and wheel,
And the worter slosh and reel
And jest ravel out in froth
Flossier'n satin cloth!
Rickollect them paddles jest
Knock the bubbles galley-west,
And plunge under, and come up
Drippin' like a worter-pup!

And to see them old things gone
That I onc't was bettin' on,
In rale p'int o' fact, I feel
kindo' like that worter-wheel--,
Sorto' drippy-like and wet
Round the eyes-- but paddlin' yet,

And in mem'ry, loafin' still
Down around old Kingry's Mill!

Joney

Had a hare-lip-- Joney had:
Spiled his looks, and Joney knowed it:
Fellers tried to bore him, bad--
But ef ever he got mad,
He kep' still and never showed it.
'Druther have his mouth all pouted
And split up, and like it wuz,
Than the ones 'at laughed about it.
Purty is as purty does!

Had to listen ruther clos't
'Fore you knowed "what he wuz givin'
You; and yet, without no boast,
Joney he wuz jest the most
Entertainin' talker livin'!
Take the Scriptur's and run through 'em,
Might say, like a' auctioneer,
And 'ud argy and review 'em
'At wuz beautiful to hear!

Hare-lip and inpediment,
Both wuz bad, and both ag'in' him--
But the old folks where he went,
'Preared like, knowin' his intent,
'Scused his mouth fer what wuz in him.
And the childern all loved Joney--
And he loved 'em back, you bet--!

Putt their arms around him-- on'y
None had ever kissed him yet!

In young company, someway,
Boys 'ud grin at one another
On the sly; and girls 'ud lay
Low, with nothin' much to say,
Er leave Joney with their mother.
Many and many a time he's fetched 'em
Candy by the paper sack,
And turned right around and ketched 'em
Makin mouths behind his back!

S'prised sometimes, the slurs he took--.
Chap said onc't his mouth looked sorter
Like a fish's mouth 'ud look
When he'd be'n jerked off the hook
And plunked back into the worter--.
Same durn feller-- it's su'prisin',
But it's facts-- 'at stood and cherred
From the bank that big babtizin'
'Pike-bridge accident occurred--!

Cherred for Joney while he give
Life to little childern drowndin'!
Which wuz fittenest to live--
Him 'at cherred, er him 'at div'
And saved thirteen lives...? They found one
Body, three days later, floated
Down the by-o, eight mile' south,
All so colored-up and bloated--
On'y knowed him by his mouth!

Had a hare-lip-- Joney had--
Folks 'at filed apast all knowed it--.
Them 'at ust to smile looked sad,
But ef he thought good er bad,
He kep' still and never showed it.
'Druther have that mouth, all pouted
And split up, and like it wuz,
Than the ones 'at laughed about it--.
Purty is as purty does!

Like His Mother Used To Make

"Uncle Jake's Place," St. Jo, Mo., 1874

"I was born in Indiany," says a stranger, lank and slim,
As us fellers in the restarunt was kindo' guyin' him,
And Uncle Jake was slidin' him another punkin pie
And a' extry cup o' coffee, with a twinkle in his eye.
"I was born in Indiany-- more'n forty year' ago--
I hain't be'n back in twenty-- and I'm workin' back'ards slow;
But I've et in ever' restarunt 'twixt here and Santy Fee,
And I want to state this coffee tastes like gittin' home, to me!"

"Pour us out another, Daddy," says the feller, warmin' up,
A-speakin' 'cost a saucerful, as Uncle tuk his cup--,
"When I seed yer sign out yander," he went on, to Uncle Jake- -,
"'Come in and git some coffee like yer mother used to make'--
I thought of my old mother, and the Posey County farm,
And me a little kid ag'in, a-hangin' in her arm,
As she set the pot: a-bilin', broke the eggs and poured 'em in--"
And the feller kindo' halted, with a trimble in his chin:

And Uncle Jake he fetched the feller's coffee back, and stood
As solemn, fer a minute, as a' undertaker would;
Then he sorto' turned and tiptoed to'rds the kitchen door-- and nex',
Here comes his old wife out with him, a-rubbin' of her specs--
And she rushes fer the stranger, and she hollers out, "It's him--!
Thank God we've met him comin'--! Don't you know, yer mother, Jim?"
And the feller, as he grabbed her, says--, "You bet I hain't forgot--
But," wipin' of his eyes, says he, "yer coffee's mighty hot!"

The Train Misser

At Union Station

'Ll where in the world my eyes has bin--
Ef I hain't missed that train ag'in!
Chuff! And whistle! And toot! And ring!
But blast and blister the dasted train--!
How it does it I can't explain!
Git here thirty-five minutes before
The durn things due--! And, drat the thing
It'll manage to git past-shore!

The more I travel around, the more
I got no sense--! To stand right here
And let it beat me! 'Ll ding my melts!
I got no gumption, ner nothin' else!
Ticket Agent's a dad-burned bore--!
Sell you a tickets all they keer--!
Ticket Agents ort to all be

Prosecuted-- and that's jes what--!
How'd I know which train's fer me?

And how'd I know which train was not--?
Goern and comin' and gone astray,
And backin' and switchin' ever'-which-way!

Ef I could jes sneak round behind
Myse'f, where I could git full swing,
I'd lift my coat, and kick, by jing!
Till I jes got jerked up and fined--!
Fer here I stood, as a durn fool's apt
To, and let that train jes chuff and choo
Right apast me-- and mouth jes gapped
Like a blamed old sandwitch warped in two!

Granny

Granny's come to our house,
And ho! My lawzy-daisy!
All the childern round the place
Is ist a-runnin' crazy!
Fetched a cake fer little Jake,
And fetched a pie fer Nanny,
And fetched a pear fer all the pack
That runs to kiss their Granny!

Lucy Ellen's in her lap,
And Wade and Silas Walker
Both's a ridin' on her foot,
And 'Pollos on the rocker;
And Marthy's twins, from Aunt Marinn's
And little Orphant Annie,
All's a-eatin' gingerbread
And giggle-un at Granny!

Tells us all the fairy tales
Ever thought er wundered--
And 'bundance o' other stories--
Bet she knows a hunderd--!

Bob's the one fer "Whittington,"
And "Golden Locks" fer Fanny!
Hear 'em laugh and clap their hands,
Listenin' at Granny!

"Jack the Giant-Killer" 's good;
And "Bean-Stalk" 's another--!
So's the one of "Cinderell'"
And her old godmother--;
That-un's best of all the rest--
Bestest one of any--,
Where the mices scampers home
Like we runs to Granny!

Granny's come to our house,
Ho! My lawzy-daisy!
All the childern round the place
Is ist a runnin' crazy!
Fetched a cake fer little Jake,
And fetched a pie fer Nanny,
And fetched a pear fer all the pack
That runs to kiss their Granny!

Old October

Old October's purt' nigh gone,
And the frosts is comin' on
Little heavier every day--
Like our hearts is thataway!
Leaves is changin' overhead
Back from green to gray and red,
Brown and yeller, with their stems
Loosenin' on the oaks and e'ms;
And the balance of the trees
Gittin' balder every breeze--
Like the heads we're scratchin' on!
Old October's purt' nigh gone.

I love Old October so,
I can't bear to see her go--
Seems to me like losin' some
Old-home relative er chum--
'Pears like sorto' settin' by
Some old friend 'at sigh by sigh
Was a-passin' out o' sight
Into everlastin' night!
Hickernuts a feller hears
Rattlin' down is more like tears
Drappin' on the leaves below--
I love Old October so!

Can't tell what it is about
Old October knock me out--!
I sleep well enough at night--
And the blamedest appetite

Ever mortal man possessed--,
Last thing et, it tastes the best--!
Warnuts, butternuts, pawpaws,
'Iles and limbers up my jaws
Fer raal service, sich as new
Pork, spareribs, and sausage, too--.
Yit fer all, they's somepin' 'bout
Old October knocks me out!

Jim

He was jes a plain ever'-day, all-round kind of a jour.,
Consumpted-lookin'-- but la!
The jokeiest, wittiest, story-tellin', song-singin', laughin'est, jolliest
Feller you ever saw!
Worked at jes coarse work, but you kin bet he was fine enough in his talk,
And his feelin's too!
Lordy! Ef he was on'y back on his bench ag'in to-day, a- carryin' on
Like he ust to do!

Any shopmate'll tell you there never was, on top o' dirt,
A better feller'n Jim!
You want a favor, and couldn't git it anywheres else--
You could git it o' him!
Most free-heartedest man thataway in the world, I guess!
Give up ever' nickel he's worth--
And ef you'd a-wanted it, and named it to him, and it was his,
He'd a-give you the earth!

Allus a reachin' out, Jim was, and a-he'ppin' some
Pore feller onto his feet--
He'd a-never a-keered how hungry he was hisse'f,

So's the feller got somepin' to eat!
Didn't make no differ'nce at all to him how he was dressed,
He ust to say to me--,
"You togg out a tramp purty comfortable in winter-time, a huntin' a job,
And he'll git along!" says he.

Jim didn't have, ner never could git ahead, so overly much
O' this world's goods at a time--.
'Fore now I've saw him, more'n onc't, lend a dollar, and haf to, more'n
likely,
Turn round and borry a dime!
Mebby laugh and joke about it hisse'f fer awhile-- then jerk his coat,
And kindo' square his chin,
Tie on his apern, and squat hisse'f on his old shoe-bench,
And go to peggin' ag'in!

Patientest feller too, I reckon, 'at ever jes natchurly
Coughed hisse'f to death!
Long enough after his voice was lost he'd laugh in a whisper and say
He could git ever'thing but his breath--
"You fellers," he'd sorto' twinkle his eyes and say,
"Is a-pilin' onto me
A mighty big debt fer that-air little weak-chested ghost o' mine to pack
Through all Eternity!"

Now there was a man 'at jes 'peared-like, to me,
'At ortn't a-never a-died!
"But death hain't a-showin' no favors," the old boss said--
"On'y to Jim!" and cried:
And Wigger, who puts up the best sewed-work in the shop--
Er the whole blame neighborhood--,
He says, "When God made Jim, I bet you He didn't do anything else that day
But jes set around and feel good!"

To Robert Burns

Sweet Singer that I loe the maist
O' ony, sin' wi' eager haste
I smacket bairn-lips ower the taste
O' hinnied sang,
I hail thee, though a blessed ghaist
In Heaven lang!

For weel I ken, nae cantie phrase,
Nor courtly airs, nor lairdly ways,
Could gar me freer blame, or praise,
Or proffer hand,
Where "Rantin' Robbie" and his lays
Thegither stand.

And sae these hamely lines I send,
Wi' jinglin' words at ilka end,
In echo o' the sangs that wend
Frae thee to me
Like simmer-brooks, wi mony a bend
O' wimplin' glee.

In fancy, as wi' dewy een,
I part the clouds aboon the scene
Where thou wast born, and peer atween,
I see nae spot
In a' the Hielands half sae green
And unforgot?

I see nae storied castle-hall,
Wi' banners flauntin' ower the wall

And serf and page in ready call,
Sae grand to me
As ane puir cotter's hut, wi' all
Its poverty.

There where the simple daisy grew
Sae bonnie sweet, and modest too,
Thy liltin' filled its wee head fu'
O' sic a grace,
It aye is weepin' tears o' dew
Wi' droopit face.

Frae where the heather bluebells fling
Their sangs o' fragrance to the Spring,
To where the lavrock soars to sing,
Still lives thy strain,
For' a' the birds are twittering
Sangs like thine ain.

And aye, by light o' sun or moon,
By banks o' Ayr, or Bonnie Doon,
The waters lilt nae tender tune
But sweeter seems
Because they poured their limpid rune
Through a' thy dreams.

Wi' brimmin' lip, and laughin' ee,
Thou shookest even Grief wi' glee,
Yet had nae niggart sympathy
Where Sorrow bowed,
But gavest a' thy tears as free
As a' thy gowd.

And sae it is we be thy name
To see bleeze up wi' sic a flame,
That a' pretentious stars o' fame
Maun blink asklent,
To see how simple worth may shame
Their brightest glent.

A New Year's Time at Willards's

1
The Hired Man Talks

There's old man Willards; an' his wife;
An' Marg'et-- S'repty's sister--; an'
There's me-- an' I'm the hired man;
An' Tomps McClure, you better yer life!

Well now, old Willards hain't so bad,
Considerin' the chance he's had.
Of course, he's rich, an' sleeps an' eats
Whenever he's a mind to: Takes
An' leans back in the Amen-seats
An' thanks the Lord fer all he makes--.
That's purty much all folks has got
Ag'inst the old man, like as not!
But there's his woman-- jes the turn
Of them-air two wild girls o' hern--
Marg'et an' S'repty-- allus in
Fer any cuttin'-up concern--
Church festibals, and foolishin'
Round Christmas-trees, an' New Year's sprees--
Set up to watch the Old Year go

An' New Year come-- sich things as these;
An' turkey-dinners, don't you know!
S'repty's younger, an' more gay,
An' purtier, an' finer dressed
Than Marg'et is-- but, lawzy-day!
She hain't the independentest!
"Take care!" old Willards used to say,
"Take care--! Let Marg'et have her way,
An' S'repty, you go off an' play
On your melodeum--!" But, best
Of all, comes Tomps! An' I'll be bound,
Ef he hain't jes the beatin'est
Young chap in all the country round!
Ef you knowed Tomps you'd like him, shore!
They hain't no man on top o' ground
Walks into my affections more--!
An' all the Settlement'll say
That Tomps was liked jes thataway
By ever'body, till he tuk
A shine to S'repty Willards--. Then
You'd ort'o see the old man buck
An' h'ist hisse'f, an' paw the dirt,
An' hint that "common workin'-men
That didn't want their feelin's hurt
'Ud better hunt fer 'comp'ny' where
The folks was pore an' didn't care--!"
The pine-blank facts is--, the old man,
Last Christmas was a year ago,
Found out some presents Tomps had got
Fer S'repty, an' hit made him hot--
Set down an' tuk his pen in hand
An' writ to Tomps an' told him so
On legal cap, in white an' black,

An' give him jes to understand
"No Christmas-gifts o' 'lily-white'
An' bear's-ile could fix matters right,"
An' wropped 'em up an' sent 'em back!
Well, S'repty cried an' snuffled round
Consid'able. But Marg'et she
Toed out another sock, an' wound
Her knittin' up, an' drawed the tea,
An' then set on the supper-things,
An' went up in the loft an' dressed--
An' through it all you'd never guessed
What she was up to! An' she brings
Her best hat with her an her shawl,
An' gloves, an' redicule, an' all,
An' injirubbers, an' comes down
An' tells 'em she's a-goin' to town
To he'p the Christmas goin's-on
Her Church got up. An' go she does--
The best hosswoman ever was!
"An" what'll We do while you're gone?"
The old man says, a-tryin' to be
Agreeable. "Oh! You?" says she--,
"You kin jaw S'repty, like you did,
An' slander Tomps!" An' off she rid!

Now, this is all I'm goin' to tell
Of this-here story-- that is, I
Have done my very level best
As fur as this, an' here I "dwell,"
As auctioneers says, winkin' sly:
Hit's old man Willards tells the rest.

2
The Old Man Talks

Adzackly jes one year ago,
This New Year's day, Tomps comes to me--
In my own house, an' whilse the folks
Was gittin' dinner--, an' he pokes
His nose right in, an' says, says he:
"I got yer note-- an' read it slow!
You don't like me, ner I don't you,"
He says--, "we're even there, you know!
But you've said, furder that no gal
Of yourn kin marry me, er shall,
An' I'd best shet off comin', too!"
An' then he says--, "Well, them's Your views--;
But havin' talked with S'repty, we
Have both agreed to disagree
With your peculiar notions-- some;
An', that s the reason, I refuse
To quit a-comin' here, but come--
Not fer to threat, ner raise no skeer
An' spile yer turkey-dinner here--,
But jes fer S'repty's sake, to sheer
Yer New Year's. Shall I take a cheer?"

Well, blame-don! Ef I ever see
Sich impidence! I couldn't say
Not nary word! But Mother she
Sot out a cheer fer Tomps, an' they
Shuk hands an' turnt their back on me.
Then I riz-- mad as mad could be--!
But Marg'et says--, "Now, Pap! You set

Right where you're settin'--! Don't you fret!
An' Tomps-- you warm yer feet!" says she,
"An throw yer mitts an' comfert on
The bed there! Where is S'repty gone!
The cabbage is a-scortchin'! Ma,
Stop cryin' there an' stir the slaw!"
Well--! What was Mother cryin' fer--?
I half riz up-- but Marg'et's chin
Hit squared-- an' I set down ag'in--
I allus was afeard o' her,
I was, by jucks! So there I set,
Betwixt a sinkin'-chill an' sweat,
An' scuffled with my wrath, an' shet
My teeth to mighty tight, you bet!
An' yit, fer all that I could do,
I eeched to jes git up an' whet
The carvin'-knife a rasp er two
On Tomps's ribs-- an' so would you--!
Fer he had riz an' faced around,
An' stood there, smilin', as they brung
The turkey in, all stuffed an' browned--
Too sweet fer nose, er tooth, er tongue!
With sniffs o' sage, an' p'r'aps a dash
Of old burnt brandy, steamin'-hot
Mixed kindo' in with apple-mash
An' mince-meat, an' the Lord knows what!
Nobody was a-talkin' then,
To 'filiate any awk'ardness--
No noise o' any kind but jes
The rattle o' the dishes when
They'd fetch 'em in an' set 'em down,
An' fix an' change 'em round an' round,
Like women does-- till Mother says--,

"Vittels is ready; Abner, call
Down S'repty-- she's up-stairs, I guess--."
And Marg'et she says, "Ef you bawl
Like that, she'll not come down at all!
Besides, we needn't wait till she
Gits down! Here Temps, set down by me,
An' Pap: say grace...!" Well, there I was--!
What could I do! I drapped my head
Behind my fists an' groaned; an' said--:
"Indulgent Parent! In Thy cause
We bow the head an' bend the knee
An' break the bread, an' pour the wine,
Feelin'--" (The stair-door suddenly
Went bang! An' S'repty flounced by me--)
"Feelin'," I says, "this feast is Thine--
This New Year's feast--" an' rap-rap-rap!
Went Marg'ets case-knife on her plate--
An' next, I heerd a sasser drap--,
Then I looked up, an' strange to state,
There S'repty set in Tomps lap--
An' huggin' him, as shore as fate!
An' Mother kissin' him k-slap!
An' Marg'et-- she chips in to drap
The ruther peert remark to me--:
"That 'grace' o' yourn," she says, "won't 'gee'--
This hain't no 'New Year's feast,'" says she--,
"This is a' Infair-Dinner, Pap!"

An' so it was--! Be'n married fer
Purt' nigh a week--! 'Twas Marg'et planned
The whole thing fer 'em, through an' through.
I'm rickonciled; an' understand,
I take things jes as they occur--,

Ef Marg'et liked Tomps, Tomps 'ud do--!
But I-says-I, a-holt his hand--,
"I'm glad you didn't marry Her--
'Cause Marg'et's my guardeen-- yes-sir--!
An' S'repty's good enough fer you!"

The Town Karnteel

The Town Karnteel--! It's who'll reveal
Its praises jushtifiable?
For who can sing av anything
So lovely and reliable?
Whin Summer, Spring, or Winter lies
From Malin's Head to Tipperary,
There's no such town for interprise
Bechuxt Youghal and Londonderry!

There's not its likes in Ireland--
For twic't the week, be gorries!
They're playing jigs upon the band,
And joomping there in sacks-- and-- and--
And racing, wid wheelborries!

Kanteel-- it's there, like any fair,
The purty gurrls is plinty, sure--!
And man-alive! At forty-five
The leg's av me air twinty, sure!
I lave me cares, and hoein' too,
Behint me, as is sinsible,
And it's Karnteel I'm goin' to,
To cilebrate in principle!

For there's the town av all the land!
And twic't the week, be-gorries!
They're playing jigs upon the band,
And joomping there in sacks-- and-- and--
And racing, wid wheelborries!

And whilst I feel for owld Karnteel
That I've no phrases glorious,
It stands above the need av love
That boasts in voice uproarious--!
Lave that for Cork, and Dublin too,
And Armagh and Killarney thin--,
And Karnteel won't be troublin' you
Wid any jilous blarney, thin!

For there's the town av all the land
Where twic't the week, be-gorries!
They're playing jigs upon the band,
And joomping there in sacks-- and-- and--
And racing, wid wheelborries!

Regardin' Terry Hut

Sence I tuk holt o' Gibbses' Churn
And be'n a-handlin' the concern,
I've travelled round the grand old State
Of Indiany, lots, o' late--!
I've canvassed Crawferdsville and sweat
Around the town o' Layfayette;
I've saw a many a County-seat
I ust to think was hard to beat:
At constant dreenage and expense
I've worked Greencastle and Vincennes--
Drapped out o' Putnam into Clay,
Owen, and on down thataway
Plum into Knox, on the back-track
Fer home ag'in-- and glad I'm back--!
I've saw these towns, as I say-- but
They's none 'at beats old Terry Hut!

It's more'n likely you'll insist
I claim this 'cause I'm prejudist,
Bein' born'd here in ole Vygo
In sight o' Terry Hut--; but no,
Yer clean dead wrong--! And I maintain
They's nary drap in ary vein
O' mine but what's as free as air
To jest take issue with you there--!
'Cause, boy and man, fer forty year,
I've argied ag'inst livin' here,
And jawed around and traded lies
About our lack o' enterprise,
And tuk and turned in and agreed

All other towns was in the lead,
When-- drat my melts--! They couldn't cut
No shine a-tall with Terry Hut!

Take even, statesmanship, and wit,
And ginerel git-up-and-git,
Old Terry Hut is sound clean through--!
Turn old Dick Thompson loose, er Dan
Vorehees-- and where's they any man
Kin even hold a candle to
Their eloquence--? And where's as clean
A fi-nan-seer as Rile' McKeen--
Er puorer, in his daily walk,
In railroad er in racin' stock!
And there's 'Gene Debs-- a man 'at stands
And jest holds out in his two hands
As warm a heart as ever beat
Betwixt here and the Jedgement Seat--!
All these is reasons why I putt
Sich bulk o' faith in Terry Hut.

So I've come back, with eyes 'at sees
My faults, at last--, to make my peace
With this old place, and truthful' swear--
Like Gineral Tom Nelson does--,
"They hain't no city anywhere
On God's green earth lays over us!"
Our city government is grand--
"Ner is they better farmin'-land
Sun-kissed--" as Tom goes on and says--
"Er dower'd with sich advantages!"
And I've come back, with welcome tread,
From journeyin's vain, as I have said,

To settle down in ca'm content,
And cuss the towns where I have went,
And brag on ourn, and boast and strut
Around the streets o' Terry Hut!

Leedle Dutch Baby

Leedle Dutch baby haff come ter town!
Jabber und jump till der day gone down--
Jabber und sphlutter und sphlit hees jaws--
Vot a Dutch baby dees Londsmon vas!
I dink dose mout' vas leedle too vide
Ober he laugh fon dot altso-side!
Haff got blenty off deemple und vrown--?
Hey! Leedle Dutchman come ter town!

Leedle Dutch baby, I dink me proud
Ober your fader can schquall dot loud
Ven he vas leedle Dutch baby like you
Und yoost don't gare, like he alvays do--!
Guess ven dey vean him on beer, you bet
Dot's der because dot he aind veaned yet--!
Vot you said off he dringk you down--?
Hey! Leedle Dutchman come ter town!

Leedle Dutch baby, yoost schquall avay--
Schquall fon preakfast till gisterday!
Better you all time gry und shout
Dan shmile me vonce fon der coffin out!
Vot I gare off you keek my nose
Downside-up mit your heels und toes--
Downside, oder der oopside-down--?

Hey! Leedle Dutchman come ter town!

Down On Wriggle Crick

"Best time to kill a hog's when he's fat." --Old Saw.

Mostly folks is law-abidin'
Down on Wriggle Crick--,
Seein' they's no Squire residin'
In our bailywick;
No grand juries, no suppeenies,
Ner no vested rights to pick
Out yer man, jerk up and jail ef
He's outragin' Wriggle Crick!

Wriggle Crick hain't got no lawin',
Ner no suits to beat;
Ner no court-house gee-and-hawin'
Like a County-seat;
Hain't no waitin' round fer verdick,
Ner non-gittin' witness-fees;
Ner no thiefs 'at gits "new heain's,"
By some lawyer slick as grease!

Wriggle Cricks's leadin' spirit
Is old Johnts Culwell--,
Keeps post-office, and right near it
Owns what's called "The Grand Hotel--"
(Warehouse now--) buys wheat and ships it;
Gits out ties, and trades in stock,
And knows all the high-toned drummers

'Twixt South Bend and Mishawauk'

Last year comes along a feller--
Sharper 'an a lance--
Stovepipe-hat and silk umbreller,
And a boughten all-wool pants--,
Tinkerin of clocks and watches:
Says a trial's all he wants--
And rents out the tavern-office
Next to Uncle Johnts.

Well--. He tacked up his k'dentials,
And got down to biz--.
Captured Johnts by cuttin' stenchils
Fer them old wheat-sacks o' his--.

Fixed his clock, in the post-office--
Painted fer him, clean and slick,
'Crost his safe, in gold-leaf letters,
"J. Culwells's Wriggle Crick."

Any kindo' job you keered to
Resk him with, and bring,
He'd fix fer you-- jest appeared to
Turn his hand to anything--!
Rings, er earbobs, er umbrellers--
Glue a cheer er chany doll--,
W'y, of all the beatin' fellers,
He Jest beat 'em all!

Made his friends, but wouldn't stop there--,
One mistake he learnt,
That was, sleepin' in his shop there--.

And one Sund'y night it burnt!
Come in one o' jest a-sweepin'
All the whole town high and dry--
And that feller, when they waked him,
Suffocatin', mighty nigh!

Johnts he drug him from the buildin',
He'pless-- 'peared to be--,
And the women and the childern
Drenchin' him with sympathy!
But I noticed Johnts helt on him
With a' extry lovin' grip,
And the men-folks gethered round him
In most warmest pardership!

That's the whole mess, grease-and-dopin'!
Johnt's safe was saved--,
But the lock was found sprung open,
And the inside caved.
Was no trial-- ner no jury--
Ner no jedge ner court-house-click--.
Circumstances alters cases
Down on Wriggle Crick!

When De Folks Is Gone

What dat scratchin' at de kitchin do'?
Done heah'n dat foh an hour er mo'!
Tell you Mr. Niggah, das sho's yo' bo'n,
Hit's mighty lonesome waitin' when de folks is gone!

Blame my trap! How de wind do blow!
An' dis is das de night foh de witches, sho'!
Dey's trouble gon' to waste when de old slut whine,
An' you heah de cat a-spittin' when de moon don't shine!

Chune my fiddle, an' de bridge go "bang!"
An' I lef' 'er right back whah she allus hang,
An' de tribble snap short an' de apern split
When dey no mortal man wah a-tetchin' hit!

Dah! Now, what? How de ole j'ice cracks!
'Spec' dis house, ef hit tell plain fac's,
'Ud talk about de ha'nts wid dey long tails on
What das'n't on'y come when de folks is gone!

What I tuk an' done ef a sho'-nuff ghos'
Pop right up by de ole bed-pos'?
What dat shinin' fru de front do' crack...?
God bress de Lo'd! Hit's de folks got back!

The Little Town O' Tailholt

You kin boast about yer cities, and their stiddy growth and size,
And brag about yer County-seats, and business enterprise,
And railroads, and factories, and all sich foolery--
But the little Town o' Tailholt is big enough fer me!

You kin harp about yer churches, with their steeples in the clouds,
And gas about yer graded streets, and blow about yer crowds;
You kin talk about yer "theaters," and all you've got to see--
But the little Town o' Tailholt is show enough fer me!

They hain't no style in our town-- hit's little-like and small--
They hain't no "churches," nuther--, jes' the meetin' house is all;
They's no sidewalks, to speak of-- but the highway's allus free,
And the little Town o' Tailholt is wide enough fer me!

Some find it discommodin'-like, I'm willin' to admit,
To hev but one post-office, and a womern keepin' hit,
And the drug-store, and shoe-shop, and grocery, all three--
But the little Town o' Tailholt is handy 'nough fer me!

You kin smile and turn yer nose up, and joke and hev yer fun,
And laugh and holler "Tail-holts is better holts'n none!
Ef the city suits you better w'y, hit's where you'd ort'o be--
But the little Town o' Tailholt's good enough fer me!

Little Orphant Annie

Little Orphant Annie's come to our house to stay,
An' wash the cups an' saucers up, an' brush the crumbs away,
An' shoo the chickens off the porch, an' dust the hearth, an' sweep,
An' make the fire, an' bake the bread, an' earn her board-an'-keep;
An' all us other childern, when the supper things is done,
We set around the kitchen fire an' has the mostest fun
A-list'nin' to the witch-tales 'at Annie tells about,
An' the Gobble-uns 'at gits you
    Ef you
      Don't
        Watch
         Out!

Onc't they was a little boy wouldn't say his prayers--,
An' when he went to bed at night, away up stairs,
His Mammy heerd him holler, an' his Daddy heerd him bawl,
An' when they turn't the kivvers down, he wasn't there at all!
An' they seeked him in the rafter-room, an' cubby-hole, an' press,
An' seeked him up the chimbly-flue, an' ever'wheres, I guess;
But all they found was thist his pants an' roundabout--:
An' the Gobble-uns 'll git you
    Ef you
      Don't
        Watch
         Out!

An' one time a little girl 'ud allus laugh and grin,
An' make fun of ever'one, an' all her blood an' kin;
An' onc't, when they was "company," an' ole folks was there,
She mocked 'em an' shocked 'em, an' said she didn't care!

An' thist as she kicked her heels, an' turn't to run an' hide,
They was two great big Black Things a-standin' by her side,
An' they snatched her through the ceilin' 'fore she knowed what she's about!
An' the Gobble-uns 'll git you
    Ef you
       Don't
          Watch
             Out!

An' little Orphant Annie says, when the blaze is blue,
An' the lamp-wick sputters, an' the wind goes woo-oo!
An' you hear the crickets quit, an' the moon is gray,
An' the lightn'-bugs in dew is all squenched away--,
You better mind yer parents, an' yer teachers fond an' dear,
An' churish them 'at loves you, an' dry the orphant's tear,
An' he'p the pore an' needy ones 'at clusters all about
Er the Gobble-uns 'll git you
    Ef you
       Don't
          Watch
             Out!

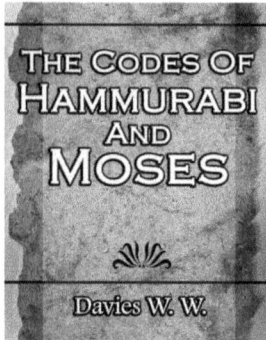

The Codes Of Hammurabi And Moses
W. W. Davies

QTY

The discovery of the Hammurabi Code is one of the greatest achievements of archaeology, and is of paramount interest, not only to the student of the Bible, but also to all those interested in ancient history...

Religion   **ISBN:** *1-59462-338-4*   **Pages:132**

MSRP $12.95

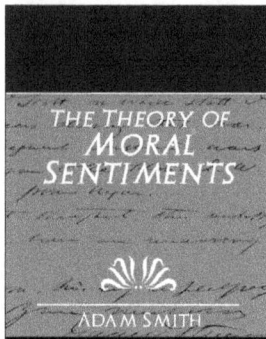

The Theory of Moral Sentiments
Adam Smith

QTY

This work from 1749. contains original theories of conscience amd moral judgment and it is the foundation for systemof morals.

Philosophy   ISBN: *1-59462-777-0*   **Pages:536**

MSRP $19.95

Jessica's First Prayer
Hesba Stretton

QTY

In a screened and secluded corner of one of the many railway-bridges which span the streets of London there could be seen a few years ago, from five o'clock every morning until half past eight, a tidily set-out coffee-stall, consisting of a trestle and board, upon which stood two large tin cans, with a small fire of charcoal burning under each so as to keep the coffee boiling during the early hours of the morning when the work-people were thronging into the city on their way to their daily toil...

Pages:84

Childrens   ISBN: *1-59462-373-2*   *MSRP $9.95*

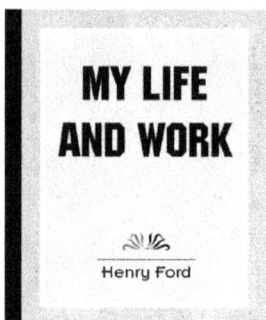

My Life and Work
Henry Ford

QTY

Henry Ford revolutionized the world with his implementation of mass production for the Model T automobile. Gain valuable business insight into his life and work with his own auto-biography... "We have only started on our development of our country we have not as yet, with all our talk of wonderful progress, done more than scratch the surface. The progress has been wonderful enough but..."

Pages:300

Biographies/   **ISBN:** *1-59462-198-5*   *MSRP $21.95*

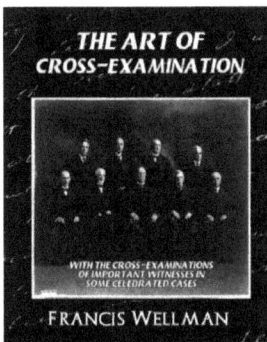

The Art of Cross-Examination
Francis Wellman

QTY

I presume it is the experience of every author, after his first book is published upon an important subject, to be almost overwhelmed with a wealth of ideas and illustrations which could readily have been included in his book, and which to his own mind, at least, seem to make a second edition inevitable. Such certainly was the case with me; and when the first edition had reached its sixth impression in five months, I rejoiced to learn that it seemed to my publishers that the book had met with a sufficiently favorable reception to justify a second and considerably enlarged edition. ..

Reference   **ISBN: *1-59462-647-2***

Pages:412

MSRP $19.95

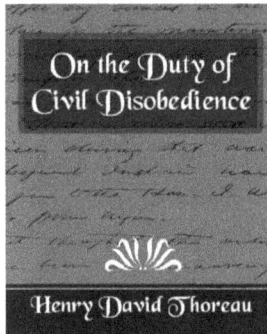

On the Duty of Civil Disobedience
Henry David Thoreau

QTY

Thoreau wrote his famous essay, On the Duty of Civil Disobedience, as a protest against an unjust but popular war and the immoral but popular institution of slave-owning. He did more than write—he declined to pay his taxes, and was hauled off to gaol in consequence. Who can say how much this refusal of his hastened the end of the war and of slavery ?

Law   **ISBN: *1-59462-747-9***

Pages:48

MSRP $7.45

Dream Psychology Psychoanalysis for Beginners
Sigmund Freud

QTY

Sigmund Freud, born Sigismund Schlomo Freud (May 6, 1856 - September 23, 1939), was a Jewish-Austrian neurologist and psychiatrist who co-founded the psychoanalytic school of psychology. Freud is best known for his theories of the unconscious mind, especially involving the mechanism of repression; his redefinition of sexual desire as mobile and directed towards a wide variety of objects; and his therapeutic techniques, especially his understanding of transference in the therapeutic relationship and the presumed value of dreams as sources of insight into unconscious desires.

Psychology   **ISBN: *1-59462-905-6***

Pages:196

MSRP $15.45

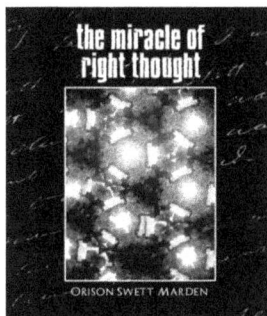

The Miracle of Right Thought
Orison Swett Marden

QTY

Believe with all of your heart that you will do what you were made to do. When the mind has once formed the habit of holding cheerful, happy, prosperous pictures, it will not be easy to form the opposite habit. It does not matter how improbable or how far away this realization may see, or how dark the prospects may be, if we visualize them as best we can, as vividly as possible, hold tenaciously to them and vigorously struggle to attain them, they will gradually become actualized, realized in the life. But a desire, a longing without endeavor, a yearning abandoned or held indifferently will vanish without realization.

Pages:360

Self Help   **ISBN: *1-59462-644-8***

MSRP $25.45

www.bookjungle.com *email: sales@bookjungle.com fax: 630-214-0564 mail: Book Jungle PO Box 2226 Champaign, IL 61825*

QTY

The Rosicrucian Cosmo-Conception Mystic Christianity by *Max Heindel* ISBN: *1-59462-188-8* **$38.95**
The Rosicrucian Cosmo-conception is not dogmatic, neither does it appeal to any other authority than the reason of the student. It is: not controversial, but is: sent forth in the, hope that it may help to clear... New Age/Religion Pages 646

Abandonment To Divine Providence by *Jean-Pierre de Caussade* ISBN: *1-59462-228-0* **$25.95**
"The Rev. Jean Pierre de Caussade was one of the most remarkable spiritual writers of the Society of Jesus in France in the 18th Century. His death took place at Toulouse in 1751. His works have gone through many editions and have been republished... Inspirational/Religion Pages 400

Mental Chemistry by *Charles Haanel* ISBN: *1-59462-192-6* **$23.95**
Mental Chemistry allows the change of material conditions by combining and appropriately utilizing the power of the mind. Much like applied chemistry creates something new and unique out of careful combinations of chemicals the mastery of mental chemistry... New Age Pages 354

The Letters of Robert Browning and Elizabeth Barret Barrett 1845-1846 vol II ISBN: *1-59462-193-4* **$35.95**
by *Robert Browning* and *Elizabeth Barrett* Biographies Pages 596

Gleanings In Genesis (volume I) by *Arthur W. Pink* ISBN: *1-59462-130-6* **$27.45**
Appropriately has Genesis been termed "the seed plot of the Bible" for in it we have, in germ form, almost all of the great doctrines which are afterwards fully developed in the books of Scripture which follow... Religion/Inspirational Pages 420

The Master Key by *L. W. de Laurence* ISBN: *1-59462-001-6* **$30.95**
In no branch of human knowledge has there been a more lively increase of the spirit of research during the past few years than in the study of Psychology, Concentration and Mental Discipline. The requests for authentic lessons in Thought Control, Mental Discipline and... New Age/Business Pages 422

The Lesser Key Of Solomon Goetia by *L. W. de Laurence* ISBN: *1-59462-092-X* **$9.95**
This translation of the first book of the "Lemegton" which is now for the first time made accessible to students of Talismanic Magic was done, after careful collation and edition, from numerous Ancient Manuscripts in Hebrew, Latin, and French... New Age/Occult Pages 92

Rubaiyat Of Omar Khayyam by *Edward Fitzgerald* ISBN:*1-59462-332-5* **$13.95**
Edward Fitzgerald, whom the world has already learned, in spite of his own efforts to remain within the shadow of anonymity, to look upon as one of the rarest poets of the century, was born at Bredfield, in Suffolk, on the 31st of March, 1809. He was the third son of John Purcell... Music Pages 172

Ancient Law by *Henry Maine* ISBN: *1-59462-128-4* **$29.95**
The chief object of the following pages is to indicate some of the earliest ideas of mankind, as they are reflected in Ancient Law, and to point out the relation of those ideas to modern thought. Religion/History Pages 452

Far-Away Stories by *William J. Locke* ISBN: *1-59462-129-2* **$19.45**
"Good wine needs no bush, but a collection of mixed vintages does. And this book is just such a collection. Some of the stories I do not want to remain buried for ever in the museum files of dead magazine-numbers an author's not unpardonable vanity..." Fiction Pages 272

Life of David Crockett by *David Crockett* ISBN: *1-59462-250-7* **$27.45**
"Colonel David Crockett was one of the most remarkable men of the times in which he lived. Born in humble life, but gifted with a strong will, an indomitable courage, and unremitting perseverance... Biographies/New Age Pages 424

Lip-Reading by *Edward Nitchie* ISBN: *1-59462-206-X* **$25.95**
Edward B. Nitchie, founder of the New York School for the Hard of Hearing, now the Nitchie School of Lip-Reading, Inc, wrote "LIP-READING Principles and Practice". The development and perfecting of this meritorious work on lip-reading was an undertaking... How-to Pages 400

A Handbook of Suggestive Therapeutics, Applied Hypnotism, Psychic Science ISBN: *1-59462-214-0* **$24.95**
by *Henry Munro* Health/New Age/Health/Self-help Pages 376

A Doll's House: and Two Other Plays by *Henrik Ibsen* ISBN: *1-59462-112-8* **$19.95**
Henrik Ibsen created this classic when in revolutionary 1848 Rome. Introducing some striking concepts in playwriting for the realist genre, this play has been studied the world over. Fiction/Classics/Plays 308

The Light of Asia by *sir Edwin Arnold* ISBN: *1-59462-204-3* **$13.95**
In this poetic masterpiece, Edwin Arnold describes the life and teachings of Buddha. The man who was to become known as Buddha to the world was born as Prince Gautama of India but he rejected the worldly riches and abandoned the reigns of power when... Religion/History/Biographies Pages 170

The Complete Works of Guy de Maupassant by *Guy de Maupassant* ISBN: *1-59462-157-8* **$16.95**
"For days and days, nights and nights, I had dreamed of that first kiss which was to consecrate our engagement, and I knew not on what spot I should put my lips..." Fiction/Classics Pages 240

The Art of Cross-Examination by *Francis L. Wellman* ISBN: *1-59462-309-0* **$26.95**
Written by a renowned trial lawyer, Wellman imparts his experience and uses case studies to explain how to use psychology to extract desired information through questioning. How-to/Science/Reference Pages 408

Answered or Unanswered? by *Louisa Vaughan* ISBN: *1-59462-248-5* **$10.95**
Miracles of Faith in China Religion Pages 112

The Edinburgh Lectures on Mental Science (1909) by *Thomas* ISBN: *1-59462-008-3* **$11.95**
This book contains the substance of a course of lectures recently given by the writer in the Queen Street Hall, Edinburgh. Its purpose is to indicate the Natural Principles governing the relation between Mental Action and Material Conditions... New Age/Psychology Pages 148

Ayesha by *H. Rider Haggard* ISBN: *1-59462-301-5* **$24.95**
Verily and indeed it is the unexpected that happens! Probably if there was one person upon the earth from whom the Editor of this, and of a certain previous history, did not expect to hear again... Classics Pages 380

Ayala's Angel by *Anthony Trollope* ISBN: *1-59462-352-X* **$29.95**
The two girls were both pretty, but Lucy who was twenty-one who supposed to be simple and comparatively unattractive, whereas Ayala was credited, as her Bombwhat romantic name might show, with poetic charm and a taste for romance. Ayala when her father died was nineteen... Fiction Pages 484

The American Commonwealth by *James Bryce* ISBN: *1-59462-286-8* **$34.45**
An interpretation of American democratic political theory. It examines political mechanics and society from the perspective of Scotsman James Bryce Politics Pages 572

Stories of the Pilgrims by *Margaret P. Pumphrey* ISBN: *1-59462-116-0* **$17.95**
This book explores pilgrims religious oppression in England as well as their escape to Holland and eventual crossing to America on the Mayflower, and their early days in New England... History Pages 268

QTY

The Fasting Cure *by Sinclair Upton*   ISBN: *1-59462-222-1*   **$13.95**
In the Cosmopolitan Magazine for May, 1910, and in the Contemporary Review (London) for April, 1910, I published an article dealing with my experiences in fasting. I have written a great many magazine articles, but never one which attracted so much attention... New Age/Self Help/Health Pages 164

Hebrew Astrology *by Sepharial*   ISBN: *1-59462-308-2*   **$13.45**
In these days of advanced thinking it is a matter of common observation that we have left many of the old landmarks behind and that we are now pressing forward to greater heights and to a wider horizon than that which represented the mind-content of our progenitors... Astrology Pages 144

Thought Vibration or The Law of Attraction in the Thought World   ISBN: *1-59462-127-6*   **$12.95**
by William Walker Atkinson   Psychology/Religion Pages 144

Optimism *by Helen Keller*   ISBN: *1-59462-108-X*   **$15.95**
Helen Keller was blind, deaf, and mute since 19 months old, yet famously learned how to overcome these handicaps, communicate with the world, and spread her lectures promoting optimism. An inspiring read for everyone... Biographies/Inspirational Pages 84

Sara Crewe *by Frances Burnett*   ISBN: *1-59462-360-0*   **$9.45**
In the first place, Miss Minchin lived in London. Her home was a large, dull, tall one, in a large, dull square, where all the houses were alike, and all the sparrows were alike, and where all the door-knockers made the same heavy sound... Childrens/Classic Pages 88

The Autobiography of Benjamin Franklin *by Benjamin Franklin*   ISBN: *1-59462-135-7*   **$24.95**
The Autobiography of Benjamin Franklin has probably been more extensively read than any other American historical work, and no other book of its kind has had such ups and downs of fortune. Franklin lived for many years in England, where he was agent... Biographies/History Pages 332

Name	
Email	
Telephone	
Address	
City, State ZIP	

☐ **Credit Card**   ☐ **Check / Money Order**

Credit Card Number	
Expiration Date	
Signature	

Please Mail to: Book Jungle
                            PO Box 2226
                            Champaign, IL 61825
or Fax to: 630-214-0564

ORDERING INFORMATION
web: *www.bookjungle.com*
email: *sales@bookjungle.com*
fax: *630-214-0564*
mail: *Book Jungle PO Box 2226 Champaign, IL 61825*
or PayPal *to sales@bookjungle.com*

Please contact us for bulk discounts

DIRECT-ORDER TERMS

**20% Discount if You Order
Two or More Books**
Free Domestic Shipping!
Accepted: Master Card, Visa,
Discover, American Express

www.ingramcontent.com/pod-product-compliance
Lightning Source LLC
Chambersburg PA
CBHW081234090426
42738CB00016B/3295